With this new volume Bühlman
and ecumenical documentary o
years this mission has been atta
tionalists, radical Christians, and atheists.

Are the missionaries really the paid servants of colonialism who cooperate in political exploitation and in the destruction of the very being of the missionized countries?

Walbert Bühlmann knows the development and the work of the missionaries and the difficulties of the situation as scarcely anybody else does.

In the exciting framework of a simulated legal court case in 1980 is reflected real history, illustrated from documents of today: the powerful drama of Christianity in Africa today. Hard accusations are made against mission and missionaries as they were and are pronounced. But the defense, too, is expressed from all points of view: in the testimonies of the Catholic and Protestant missionaries who without exaggeration, soberly, self-critically and for that very reason convincingly, report on their active work and their life.

The reader will follow this ecumenical documentation with excitement, interest, and ever-growing sympathy. It succeeds in imparting a just and comprehensive picture of the reality of the African mission today.

Walbert Bühlmann, O.F.M. Cap. (photograph: back cover) was a missionary in Tanganyika. From 1954 to 1970 he taught missiology at Freiburg University, Switzerland, and edited missionary journals. He was professor at the Gregorian University in Rome. Since 1971 he has been secretary general for the Capuchin missions throughout the world. Among his principal publications are *The Coming of the Third Church*, published in five languages, and *Courage, Church!*

Cover design: R. Klein (reproduced by courtesy of Verlag Knecht)
Photos: J.A. Stolz (front). J.Gürer (back)

By the same author

The Coming of the Third Church
An Analysis of the Present and Future of the Church

Courage, Church!
Essays in Ecclesial Spirituality

Walbert Bühlmann OFM Cap.

The Missions on Trial

Addis Ababa 1980

A moral for the future from the archives of today

Maryknoll, New York 10545

1979

Original title: *Missionsprozess in Addis Abeba*. Copyright © 1977 by Verlag Josef Knecht, Carolusdruckerei Gmbh., Frankfurt am Main. Translated from the German by A.P. Dolan, assisted by B. Krokosz.

The Catholic Foreign Mission Society of America (Maryknoll) recruits and trains people for overseas missionary service. Through Orbis Books Maryknoll aims to foster the international dialogue that is essential to mission. The books published, however, reflect the opinions of their authors and are not meant to represent the official position of the Society.

Library of Congress Cataloging in Publication Data

Bühlmann, Walbert.
The missions on trial-Addis Ababa, 1980.

Translation of Missionsprozess in Addis Abeba.
Bibliography: p.
1. Missions—Africa—Influence. I. Title.
BV3500.B8313 1979 266'.0096 78-23922
ISBN 0-88344-316-3

First published in Great Britain October 1978.

U. S. edition, 1979, Orbis Books, Maryknoll, NY 10545

Manufactured in the United States of America

CONTENTS

M.P. Hegba: "What we wish for is a long moratorium in which we will be left alone with our God, so that his Spirit can visit us — without intermediaries and witnesses, without having to request permission from some distant authority; so that his light can enlighten us — without having . . . to pass through the prism of a foreign culture." [53]

H. Müller: (The missionaries) "in order to impress sentimental people, (depicted in their magazines) — in a dozen different ways — the outstretched hands of sick, leprous, deformed or starving beggars . . . instead of showing us the convincing power of (African) culture." [58]

B. Mongo: (The African writers) "regard the Church as an organisation rather than a body pulsating with holiness . . . The dynamism of the Sermon on the Mount is in harsh contrast to the brutality and day-to-day godlessness of the white Christians." [61]

H.W. Mobley: "Instead of asking for hospitality from the African religions, Christianity . . . has driven the inhabitants out of their own house, and the missionaries, like iconoclasts, have smashed the African religion to pieces." [65]

Bishop J. Blomjous: "We all were and we remain always children of our time. One can in retrospect judge the attitudes of earlier generations but one cannot simply condemn them without more ado." [71]

F. Raaflaub: "The very unpretentious village school (run by the missionaries) started a process which could never be arrested — the awakening of Africa." [79]

Sr J. Delaney: "Dr Schweitzer and Dr Goarnisson are only two prominent tips of an iceberg. All the other (doctors and nurses) are not exposed to publicity; the thanks they receive is the shining eyes of those they have healed." [86]

Sr Marie-André: "Nowadays African women play a quite considerable role in modern society . . . In order to appreciate this remarkable development properly we must turn back the pages of history several decades." [90]

H. Huber: "What I would do would be to remove (from a library dealing exclusively with Africa) all the books on linguistics, ethnology and culture written by Catholic or Protestant missionaries; then one would see with one's own eyes that the contents of that library had been halved." [96]

U. Fick: "In Africa at the present time there are 78 interconfessional translations or revisions of the Bible under way, a development which even optimists could never have foreseen." [100]

P.R. Clifford: (The story of Africa's development) "is the work of men of flesh and blood, men endowed with courage and hope . . . men and women who have risked everything to proclaim the Gospel . . . and have built for Africa the foundations of a new era." [103]

A. Thielemeier: "The attitude of the African people to these foreigners was humane and welcoming, but the country and its climate were dreadful. Heroism and supernatural motivation were required to survive the early stages and finally to reach the present point of development." [110]

E.A. Ayandale: "A further consideration which might help to exonerate the missions as an institution is the fact that the missionary message really had a deep revolutionary effect and that present-day Africa would never have come into being had it not been for this ferment." [119]

Foreword

The missions in Africa have for many years been in the crossfire of criticism. In an earlier age they were much admired, but nowadays they are attacked and accused — by radical Christians, by cold atheists and by black nationalists. An objective judgement is long overdue.

Anyone who knows even a little about the missions is of course aware that criticism of the missions is nothing new. Already in the writings of A. Miller and A. Heim [1] one could perceive clearly ill-will towards the missions. It is also true that there were accounts of the missions which portrayed their achievements and their lasting greatness in a positive light.[2] Nevertheless, apart from the fact that these accounts appear, nowadays at any rate, somewhat triumphalistic, they had a perhaps too academic intent and hence were read only by specialists and by active supporters of the missions, who really never doubted their greatness.

In order to avoid the problems arising from such descriptions, we have chosen to write this book in the form of political fiction, that is to say, a 'historical' account which is projected into the future, but is based upon data from the past. The aim of this technique is to bring to

[1] A. Miller, *Völkerentartung unter dem Kreuz,* Leipzig[2] 1936; A. Heim, *Weltbild eines Naturforschers,* Zürich 1942.

[2] R. Streit, *Die Weltmission der katholischen Kirche,* Hünfeld 1928; L. Berg, *Die katholische Heidenmission als Kulturträger,* Aachen 1923; F. Dessauer (ed.), *Wissen und Bekenntnis,* Olten 1944 (Antwort auf A. Heim); J. Beckmann, *Die katholische Kirche im neuen Afrika,* Einsiedeln 1947.

life documents housed in archives and to make free use of them in a way which — so we dare to hope — will arouse in the reader excitement and interest. The footnotes will constantly remind him that only the setting is imaginary; the picture itself is factual. It is the story of the powerful drama of Christianity in the Africa of today and our aim is to present it, not in a cold, academic way but in such a way that the reader can enter into the story as it develops and come to understand it more clearly. This union of fact and phantasy is closer, perhaps, than one might think to the reality of life, threaded through as it always is with mystery.

In this 'historical' account weighty accusations are formulated against the missions and against the missionaries. Even with all their exaggerations these accusations will be allowed to stand because in reality such accusations have been made and continue to be made, and we must not pretend that this is not so. After that, the case for the defence will be presented, but without arrogance and in a spirit of sobriety and self-criticism which, for this very reason, will be convincing.

These African missionaries are fellow-citizens of ours and fellow-Christians, a part of us, and so, in reading their encouraging and at the same time depressing story, we are reading part of our own story. Imperfect like the missionaries, we too stand on trial. We will be fully satisfied only when God's kingdom, which has been promised and is quietly growing, casts its light upon history and brings it to completion.

Fr Walter Bühlmann, OFMCap.

Rome, Easter 1977.

Background

In the summer of 1979 the mood in the headquarters of the Organisation for African Unity (O.A.U.) in Addis Ababa was unlike anything that had been experienced there since 1963 when the O.A.U. was founded. For 1979 marked the final victory of the African freedom movements.

In 1965 President Julius Nyerere gave his celebrated address in Holland. Who, apart from the Africans, would have thought that the plan he outlined on that occasion would be realised so quickly? In his speech, Nyerere challenged the Western powers to do everything they could towards the peaceful liberation of the as-yet-unfree parts of Southern Africa. "If this is not achieved — God forbid! — then all of us together will have failed", he said. And he went on: "But we Africans will not be able to let things remain in that state; we will be compelled to free the Portuguese colonies by non-peaceful means. Were that to be the case, presumably the Western powers would not support us. If we were then to get help in other ways, and we would have to do so — I repeat, we would *have* to do so — then the West would not understand us. But we beg the West not to allow things to reach that stage. We beg the West to understand us now, while there is still time".

The West did not understand Nyerere and didn't lift a finger. The Western press made fun of him and said he would do better to stay at home and champion the cause of right there instead of causing trouble abroad. For this reason, things had to happen 'in other ways', and they did, one after another, with the inevitability of a clock running down.

China got a foothold in Tanzania, built the railway right up to the front-line in Rhodesia and trained the Frelimo fighters, who then in a tough guerilla war overcame the Portuguese army and liberated Mozambique. The same thing happened in Angola with the extensive involvement at the finish of Russia and Cuba. After this Rhodesia was offered the opportunity of negotiating for peace. These negotiations broke down in spite of the fact that Henry Kissinger had said quietly to Ian Smith: "The game is lost" and had publicly proclaimed — alas, ten years too late! — that "The United States of America are on the side of freedom". So, once again, war broke out. And, once again, as in Angola, the war ended with the collapse and disorganised flight of the whites who withdrew to South Africa. The same pattern was repeated in South West Africa.

In the final stage Russia got the better of China because it was able to provide more effective military assistance. Quietly and systematically it had built up its positions by putting great numbers of its ships in the Indian Ocean, by establishing military bases in Ethiopia and deep-dock harbours in Porto Amelia, Nacala, Beira and Maputo in Mozambique; in the Southern Atlantic it established bases in Guinea, Congo-Brazzaville and Angola. Russia was now getting ready for the last and toughest fight — against South Africa. Was South Africa going at last to accept majority rule and thereby defuse the situation? Or would, in this case too, force have to be the deciding factor? What a terrifying force that would be!

For the moment things were at a standstill. The victories gained up to this point were being celebrated with congratulatory messages, with speeches and with reports. During a break in the ceremonies, one member of a group talking in the lobby observed that basically he was not entirely happy about the overwhelming presence of Russia:

"We'll end up becoming Russian satellites in military and economic matters", he said. Looking slyly at some of his colleagues another rejoined: "If we ever reach that stage, have no fear, we'll shake the Russian Bear from our backs just like the Egyptians did". "Are you so self-centred that you can see only your own little country?" interposed a third man with vigour; "We need Russia's help not simply in order to get our hands on the world's gold in South Africa, we also need to get hold of the industrial diamonds and the chromium we can't do without for steel alloy and therefore for the making of weapons. As well as that, we shall have to control the oil-traffic round the Cape. We will then be able to impose a blockade on the Nato countries and in this way force the capitalist world to its knees without war. Only then will we have reached our goal and achieved a complete victory". At this point the bell called the gentlemen back into the assembly hall.

The president of the assembly had invited all the heads of state and the ministers to a 'brain-storming session' on the final afternoon, that is, a session in which all the angles and problems which might arise in the near or distant future could be discussed. The intention behind this was to avoid simply being carried away by events and to be prepared to meet and deal with them.

In the euphoric atmosphere of those days of celebrations the discussion got under way very quickly.

"In my opinion, we have left the problem of African culture too much in the hands of poets and artists. We as governments ought to give our people more help to become aware of their own identity and to make their own distinctive contribution in all areas of life instead of just copying other nations . . ."

"Even though London, Paris and Brussels are no longer the centres of our world, we are culturally still dependent on them and economically too we are at their mercy. We have to develop new initiatives in the deadlocked discussions between North and South and we must exert more pressure . . ."

"Yes, but in order to do that we must be united both regionally and as a continent. We ought really to be able to provide Europe with a model of unity as it makes its weary way towards that goal . . ."

"Let's start in a practical way with the most immediate problems. I frequently drive from Wagadugu to Lagos by way of Accra and on this journey I have to change from one side of the road to the other three times. A situation like that has often been the cause of fatal accidents . . ."

"Gentlemen, let's be honest with ourselves. Africa has a population of some 300 million, which is six times that of France or England. But Africa is made up of roughly 50 states, and so there are roughly 50 armies, 50 administrations with ministers and ministries and 50 sets of diplomatic representatives all over the world. Can a poor continent like ours permit itself such a luxury? Ordinary commonsense demands that we find, sooner or later, a more sensible solution to the problem . . ."

"The Charter of the O.A.U. provides for the neutrality of the member-states and hence for the freedom of the group as a whole. Now we see developing more and more not simply a friendship with, but an exclusive preference for, the countries of the East or of the West and this has grave political and economic consequences. More and more the super-powers are interfering in questions which concern us. Shouldn't we be resisting the movement to end our freedom as a group? Africa has an important role to play in keeping the balance of power on this planet. Are we to give up this role? . . ."

"I would like to put forward for your consideration what Ki-Zerbo says on the last page of his *History of Africa*. (I quote), 'We can live without an ideology, but we cannot speed up the course of history without one.

Until now, Africa has been governed more often than not by negative ideologies — anti-colonialism, anti-neo-colonialism, and so on. This will not do in the future. We must work out a positive ideology which will bring together under one roof the individual and collective aims of our life and will be more than a mere repetition of formulas imported from abroad'. This, I submit, should be taken very seriously . . ."

"Without wishing to reject the suggestions that have been made so far, I believe that we should investigate thoroughly the question of the missions. Are they a blessing or a burden? We cannot wipe them out from our past: the question is, can we do without them in the future? . . ."

"The language problem is clamouring for a solution. We can't go on for ever regarding French, English and Portuguese as 'our' languages. How can, I would like to ask, Arabic, Swahili and a few other languages be spread out over a wider area? . . ."

"Wait a minute! I would ask you to give the last suggestion but one further consideration. For me too, the 'foreign missions' are a thorn in the flesh. Here and there missionaries have been expelled either individually or in groups. Ought we to further this policy? . . ."

"In my view, Christianity in Africa comes and goes in waves. The first wave, in North Africa, was completely wiped out by Islam. The second wave, in the Congo and some other countries, has also ebbed. The third wave began over a hundred years ago. It is not correct to say that it has completely vanished yet, but Christianity has definitely passed its high-water mark and we will soon have our African religions back again . . ."

"Do you really think so? In my opinion, modern man no longer has to turn to religion. Religion and all its dogmas were nursery-tales for children, opium for the poor and the helpless. We have to let men be men and nothing more than men. Men will create for themselves a better world, which will not be that of the spirits and gods. This is why I personally am in favour of a radical solution to the problem . . ."

"Perhaps, but we cannot overlook the fact that, without the missions, we would not be what we are. It is not right that we should suddenly rise up against them like naughty children against their parents. It would be unjust to drive the missions out into the wilderness as a scapegoat, which is what we did with colonialism . . ."

"I move that we give the missions a proper trial, bring them before a court, a kind of people's court. Then we'll see their worth and what attitude we should take to them . . ."

"I propose an amendment. Here in Africa the people has never been the same thing as a mob; it has always known how to conduct its business in an orderly fashion according to unwritten laws. Particular attention has always been paid to the council of elders. I propose, therefore, that this trial be conducted before a council of elders. We are dealing with a very special kind of case. It is not an individual who is on trial but an institution and many members of this institution already lie buried in African soil. For a case like this there are no laws; only elders are competent to deal with such a case . . ."

"Well said! In 1980 we will be celebrating the 20th anniversary of Africa Year. It was in 1960 that 17 African states achieved their independence. The 20th anniversary of this event would provide a fitting backdrop for this trial. The white man's building in Africa had two domes, colonialism and the missions. The first of these has collapsed, but not the second — it has survived. The question is, should it continue to survive and if so, in what way? . . ."

Everyone felt this was a good idea, and the assembly drew up a general outline-plan and entrusted the secretariat with the task of putting it into operation. 1980 was going to experience a new kind of court-case altogether.

* * *

In the secretariat of the O.A.U. lots of cola-nuts were being chewed. But there were lots of other nuts to crack as well: who to invite, how to invite, where to find suitable elders?

Once the secretariat had a fairly clear idea of how things were going to run, a press-conference was held at which the purpose and mode of procedure of the forthcoming trial were explained. The reaction of the world's press varied from scepticism to cynicism. Only a handful of reporters had enough confidence in the Africans to hope for an objective trial. The christian press tried to put things in the best possible light so as not to spoil their chances before the game had begun.

The idea was that anyone could apply to speak for the prosecution or for the defence. No personal invitations or summonses were issued.

The Vatican and the World Council of Churches resolved to leave the whole affair in the hands of their African colleagues. There was no desire to boycott the trial as a matter of principle, because it might provide an opportunity to show the work of the christian missions in their true colours. More than anything else, the Churches were agreed that the defence must be coordinated and that they must accept as a body the responsibility for what was good and for what was not so good in all the missions. The scandal of division between the Churches, which had in fact done so much harm in Africa, would now have to be finally interred. Apart from these basic considerations, everything was left to the Council of the Episcopal Conferences of Africa and Madagascar whose headquarters are in Accra and to the Committee of the All Africa Churches Conference based in Nairobi.

As the opening-date of the trial drew nearer, the more it was talked about in Africa; fears were expressed as well as hopes. Here and there tensions between African and missionary clergy which until now had lain dormant came to the surface. Some African priests and politicians found it difficult to conceal their malicious delight. The missionaries, used to putting up with many hardships, didn't react to this and carried on with their work as before. They felt in their bones that the people were on their side and out of loyalty to the people they were prepared to stick it out and overlook a lot of things.

* * *

Three months before the trial began, the names of the members of the council of elders were announced.

Mr. Sinajina from Tanzania had been chosen as President. In spite of his age — he was about 75 — he was in possession of all his mental and bodily faculties. The story goes that at the end of the First World War an English officer saw this tall young man, looked him up and down, perhaps with a view to obtaining his services as a soldier, and asked him, "What do they call you?" "Sinajina", replied the young man evasively (which means "I have no name"). The officer carefully wrote in his notebook the name of this man without a name amid the sniggers of the other boys. Ever since 'Sinajina' has kept his name! Sinajina never went to school, but he got a job as cook to an Englishman and acquired a good knowledge of his master's language as well as picking up the three Rs. After his marriage he grew corn and bananas for his own use and coffee to sell. Although his tribe had converted to Christianity and although he personally had a great respect for Christians, he himself never became one. He was one of those men who are esteemed and loved by young and old alike, a rare breed, never numerous and nowadays almost extinct. Tierno Bokar from Mali belonged to this group; he was known as 'man of God', 'God's mouthpiece', 'Mali's own Francis of Assisi'.[1] A man like Sinajina was just the man for the job of President of the council of elders.

JOSEPH KI-ZERBO from Upper Volta was chosen from the short list as first Vice-President. He was a Catholic of about 60 years of age. He had worked his way up the ladder beginning as a farmer; next he was a teacher, then he became successively a reporter, a student at the Sorbonne, first president of the Union of African Catholic Students in France, founder of the periodical *Tam Tam*, lecturer at a number of high-schools in France and Africa, member or chairman of various commissions of the United Nations Organisation and of Unesco, delegate to the National Assembly and Secretary-General of the National Party in Upper Volta. He achieved particular fame with his 700-page *History of Africa*, the first history of Africa to be written by an African.[2]

The second Vice-President was to be CHRISTIAN BAETA from Ghana. A Presbyterian, he was held in high esteem in the World Council of Churches. In the fifties he had headed a group which was studying the question of the Protestant pastors in Africa and in 1954 he had published a report about it. In 1965 he headed the International Africa Seminar in Ghana and published the papers given there in book-form. For many years he was also a professor at and director of the Institute for Religious Sciences at the University of Ghana as well as being President of the International Missionary Council until the time this was incorporated into the World Council of Churches. At the

[1] Cf. Amadou Hampaté Ba, in the Foreword to G. Dieterlen, *Textes sacrés de l'Afrique Noire* (Gallimard 1965), p. 7.

[2] The bibliographical details of the authors mentioned in the text are to be found in the Bibliography.

time of his appointment to the council of elders he was leading a retired life in Ghana.

The remaining members of the council were drawn from various regions, religions and professions. There were two representatives of the new breed of farmers, two women involved in adult education, two ministers of the interior who came as witnesses and not as politicians — this was because the principle of the separation of powers was observed — and, finally, five illiterate men and women. These latter were chosen in spite of their lack of formal education because they were, after all, made in the image of God and, like Adam, could give things their proper names. The organising committee had made a very good choice of members for the council of elders, that no one could deny.

The Trial begins . . .

The great day has arrived. Over the past few days planes from Eastern, Southern, Central and Western Africa and from Europe and America have been bringing to Addis Ababa participants in the trial — speakers for the prosecution and for the defence with their camp-followers and supporters and a great gang of newspaper, radio and television reporters.

The opening was planned for Whit Tuesday, May 27; this was to commemorate the founding of the O.A.U. by 31 African heads of state in the last week of May 1963. Addis Ababa was about to witness the most spectacular event in its almost 3,000 years and the whole city was alive with expectation at what might happen.

Tuesday, May 27

Soon after eight o'clock in the morning the guests begin to make their way across Mexico Square and along the Ethiopian Monopoly up to the building of the Economic Commission for Africa with its huge Africa Hall. Everyone wants to make sure of a place because the word has got round that even this hall will be too small for all the would-be participants.

In fact, Africa Hall is full to bursting-point. On the stroke of ten trumpets erupt into wild rhythms and the 13 elders in their flowing, colourful robes enter the hall. Spotlights come on, flash-bulbs pop. Step by step a mob of photographers is forced back. The judges take their seats at the oval table and gradually the excitement dies down.

Now the President rises. Calmly he looks at the crowd and begins to speak. His sentences flow on, unhurriedly but powerfully, like the great rivers of Africa.

"Citizens of Africa! Citizens of the world! We are gathered here on the roof of Africa some 7,500 feet above the sea. Our concern is not a family quarrel but a question which occupies the minds of all thinking men and women. Africa and the world are looking at us. Let us not forget this!

"Twenty years ago the hour of freedom struck for Africa. Since then much has changed. Our capital cities are linked with the rest of the world by plane and by TV satellites. We have achieved our own identity: formerly we were European colonies, now we are on a par with the rest of the world. In this period of time the Churches too — so my christian colleagues inform me — have undergone far-reaching changes; one has only to think of the Second Vatican Council and the Plenary Assemblies of the World Council of Churches in Uppsala and Nairobi.

"We Africans have to ask ourselves: What will happen in the next 20 years? What will Africa be like in the year 2000? Should we let events take their course or should we influence them? Our past was characterised by colonialism and by the missions. The colonial system has collapsed and from its ruins our states blossomed forth. Isn't it about time for the missions to die or to be put out of the way so that we can have our own life? The history faculties of our national universities are in the process of researching the history of the last 100 years and they are bringing to light many aspects of which the whites are unaware. The whites wrote the history of their undertakings in Africa; we are writing the history of our reactions to these undertakings and, as a result, we are coming to see things which give a different impression even of the missions.

"We have been entrusted with the task of trying the missions, of establishing their positive and negative points and of asking ourselves whether the liberation movements should not also include liberating ourselves from the missions. We must never forget, however, that the liberation movements are political, the missions are religious; they are on different levels. Whatever secondary motives the missionaries may have had, their main motive for coming to Africa was religious zeal — they believed they were sent by God. Now we have a saying to the effect that, 'What God has given, the wind cannot take away'. At all events we must tackle this question with the necessary reverence, just as when he enters a church or a mosque, even the infidel takes off his shoes if only out of a sense of propriety.

"Moreover we cannot eradicate the missions even if we would like to; our country bears their stamp. Wherever one travels in Africa, one comes across mission-stations with their churches, schools and hospitals. Even though in most African countries the schools have been taken over by the state and have been given secular names, the school buildings and the hospitals built by the missionaries remain standing and future generations will know and ought to know who built them.

"We have to conduct this trial with justice and equity. It is a special kind of trial. We are not conducting a family wrangle in which the participants have taken sides before the trial has begun, we are dealing with a case in which — as can be seen from the list of those who have offered to give evidence — there are no such boundaries. It is not long since the white man was judge in Africa. Now white men face trial before black judges. White men and black are accusing white men before black men; white men and black are defending white men before black men. We are witnessing a meaningful example of Article 2 of the Human Rights Declaration of 1948, which states that all men have the same rights irrespective of race or religion. What alone is at issue is to show whether the missions are justified or not.

"We cannot be guided by the rules of the tribal courts nor of international law. The fact that the accused are not individual, concrete men but an institution makes the case a difficult one. Moreover, a good number of the members of this institution are not present. They lived at a time when the only way of getting from place to place in Africa was on foot. They are buried in Africa and so have become for ever a part of us. In this situation all I can do is to rely on the wisdom and good sense of my colleagues to find a way through this jungle. We have no public prosecutors and no officially-appointed counsel for the defence. All who have asked to do so have the right to speak. In a tribal court all the members know one another and the proceedings are accordingly more relaxed. Everyone has his say and so a common solution is reached. There is no urgency. For us Africans time is made for man and not vice-versa, but in the case we are trying, many people are short of time. The world too, which is following this trial, is suffering from lack of time. And so we have to speed things up. We cannot envisage more than a week for the prosecution and another week for the defence. For this reason we beg speakers not to waste words but only to say what is important.

"Now I have a special announcement for the ladies and gentlemen of the press. We value highly your presence here. You are our mouthpiece. Your voice carries further than do our African drums. You will help this trial to achieve the importance due to it. The world should know how Africa is thinking. But we know the strengths and the weaknesses of the mass media. After a few days they lose interest in an issue; it is only fresh events which draw their interest. For this reason the council of elders has resolved that the press should not be admitted until the case for the prosecution has been completed".

The audience is amazed to hear this. Some people interrupt, others protest or utter cries of disapproval. Only after a pause of some length is the President able to resume.

"I repeat: the press will not be admitted until the case for the prosecution is complete. The reason we have decided this is to avoid an imbalance between a lengthy reporting of the prosecution and a summary account of the defence. In the view of the council of elders, this would not be fair and no matter what the verdict may turn out to be, the missions should be given fair treatment. When the case for the defence begins, the text of all the speeches made for the prosecution will be released to the press, who can then communicate them together with the speeches for the defence. This session is now concluded".

That was a great surprise. The prosecution and the press are annoyed, the defence and the missionaries relieved.

The Case for the PROSECUTION

Wednesday, May 28

Africa Hall is not as full as it was yesterday. The press gallery is empty and there are fewer spectators. The missionaries are in a rather sombre mood.

The President (opening the meeting): "Ladies and gentlemen, our work is now about to begin. We have reduced it somewhat in that the council has rejected a number of applications to speak in order to avoid unnecessary repetitions. Our first speaker is Mrs Ofelia Tembe from the People's Republic of Mozambique. She is secretary to the editor of the magazine *Tempo*".

Ofelia Tembe[3]: "Mr President, I could present you with an account of the last 400 or of the last 40 years; it would make no difference to the degree of anger which we present-day Mozambiquans feel or of humiliation which those responsible for this period feel. It is almost 500 years since Portugal conceived the megalomaniac idea of treating the newly-discovered world of Africa and Asia as its own property which it would be able to dominate and exploit at will. Vasco da Gama, enticed by reports

[3] The text is made up from Ki-Zerbo, *Histoire*, pp. 302-306, 543-548 and various numbers of the periodical *Tempo* (C.P. 2917, Maputo, Mozambique). The second part of the text is based mainly on the article *Assimilaçao cega da cultura hebráica fundada no fanatismo religioso cristao*, which appeared in *Tempo*, September 12, 1976, pp. 33ff.

of the golden land of Monomotapa, landed in the sheltered harbour of Mozambique in 1498. An old man was forced under torture to say what he knew of this golden land. That is how it began, and that is how it has continued until the last few decades — exploitation of trade, vast estates owned by the Portuguese adventurers who behaved like kings, forced labour, epidemics, reprisals. The result is that after so many centuries we have a people robbed of their dignity and energy; 80 per cent of them illiterate. It is a long story of failure. Portugal was too small to rule so large an empire; it suffered constantly from shortage of breath.

"In spite of this, Portugal had a strong christian sense of mission or, rather, of superiority and this sense of superiority was heightened in 1493 by a Bull of Pope Alexander VI. In this Bull the whole of the New World was 'by the authority of almighty God which We enjoy, given for all time to the Spanish and Portuguese kings and their successors so that the barbarian peoples in these lands may be reduced to submission and led to the Faith'. Doesn't it make you blush, ladies and gentlemen, when you read texts like that? The christian *prazeros*, using Christianity as a cover, permitted themselves every form of cruelty. Even as late as the beginning of the 19th century 25,000 slaves were being exported every year. As a consolation prize they were baptised before they departed! The only black people who had any chance of a comfortable life were the girls, who captivated the white masters by their beauty and were taken as concubines.

"At last in 1962 the Frelimo was founded to free the people from slavery, and the Portuguese government had the nerve to emphasise — so much that nearly everyone believed them — that Mozambique was a free, peaceful and prosperous country and that if the rafters were beginning to smoulder, it was only because foreign agents, that is, Communists, were trying to set the place on fire! The bishops played the same tune, declaring that the Frelimo were rebels and that those who cooperated with them were guilty of grave sin. The bishops were all blind and remained, until after the overthrow of the government, true servants of the colonialist regime and a disgrace to the Catholic Church . . ."

Interruptions: "What about Bishop Lamont of Umtali, who hid guerillas in his house and for doing so was sentenced by the Rhodesian government to ten years in prison and then expelled?"

The President: "Interruptions will not be permitted. In the second stage there will be time enough for the defence".

Renewed interruptions: "What about the bishops of Madagascar and Tanganyika who, as early as 1953, in a pastoral letter demanded as a natural right the people's right to self-rule?"

The President: "I repeat: interruptions will not be permitted. If they continue, I shall use my authority and have the offenders removed from the hall".

Ofelia Tembe: "Please do not try to distract our attention. I'm talking about Mozambique. The fact that here and there in Africa there have been a few individual bishops or groups of bishops who were enlightened does not alter the other fact that the bishops in our country were asleep or, rather, that they cooperated actively with the government against the liberation movement. The only bishop who would have nothing to do with this kind of attitude was Manuel Vieira Pinto of Nampula: he, together with a number of non-Portuguese missionaries who had recognised the signs of the times, took official action against the 'Church' and, in return, were faced with difficulties created by the hierarchy and by the government and even with expulsion. A Church like that has made a fool of itself for good and all.

"The President of Mozambique, Samora Machel, has said repeatedly in speeches he has made since we achieved independence, 'Where was the Church when the Frelimo was fighting for liberation? It wasn't anywhere. But wait, it was; it was on the side of colonialism. Now that colonialism has disappeared, the Church should do likewise'. Or again, 'The Church divided our people into Christians and pagans, into Catholics and many kinds of Protestants. The Frelimo has united them again. For this reason the people should not listen to the Church any more but to the Frelimo'. He also said, 'In Mozambique there are so many Catholics and Protestants. How is that possible? Their body lives in Mozambique, but their head whom they obey lives in Rome or London or somewhere in the United States. This is ridiculous: a citizen of Mozambique should obey the authorities in Mozambique'. It is a proof of the President's wisdom that later on he did not repeat these accusations but left them unaltered.

"We could have brought all the bishops and many Christians before a people's court and they wouldn't have fared well, but the government was generous and instead allowed them to withdraw with dignity. Since then, something has happened very quickly which would not have been possible under Portuguese rule, viz., the Portuguese bishops have been replaced by Mozambiquans. The People's Republic of Mozambique recognises even in the constitution freedom of religion and guarantees every citizen the right to practise a religion or not as he wishes. We respect man in his freedom.

"Of course, in principle we are convinced that religion is a relic of the past and that people must be freed from it, irrespective of whether it be African, Islamic, or Christian; time itself will take care of that. Being a Christian or being an atheist is, in the end, not all that important; a Frelimo supporter is judged, not by his atheism or by his belief in God, but by the part he plays in the revolution. What cannot be reckoned as of no account is religious obscurantism, which makes people stupid and keeps them in a state of superstition, and religious fanaticism, which is divisive.

"Religious fanaticism is a sickness, it is as blind as a train going at full speed without a driver. Fanatics are not objective; they do not analyse the real facts of a situation; all they do is defend their own positions which they equate with eternal and unchanging truths. They are, therefore, men with closed minds who allow the wind to blow from one direction only.

"Believing Christians, moreover, are proud to let their banners wave in this one wind. The poorer they are in intellect, the more fanatical they are. Whenever they are confronted by atheists, they reply in set formulas and entrench themselves in their reactionary attitude. They haven't the courage to open themselves to intellectual discussion. They regard the Bible as a sacred, untouchable book written by men under divine inspiration. But we know that the biblical writers were partisans and simply defended their own cause. The Jews were a small and materially poor race and so they got bigger and bigger ideas about themselves. They developed faith in a God of the Covenant and regarded themselves as the Chosen People, raised high above all other peoples. This is how religious fanaticism came into being and it spread from Judaism to the christian Church. All the inconsistencies in what they call 'Sacred Scripture' are glossed over cheerfully and they are able to give a religious meaning even to the crass eroticism of the Song of Songs. Everything is explained in such a way as to serve the interests of the Church and of its leaders. In this way Christ has served even the lust for power of the Spaniards and Portuguese, the English and the French, and the whites in South Africa and Rhodesia. The ignorance of the Christians in Mozambique must be seen in this wider context. The Church has always encouraged obscurantism in order to be able to dominate the lowly and the humble.

"Mr President, I leave it to you and to your council to draw conclusions from these remarks".

* * *

The President: "It is now the turn of Okot p'Bitek of Uganda. He read education at Bristol, law at Aberystwyth, social anthropology at Oxford and he is at present on the staff of Nairobi University. He has to his credit a number of scholarly and political works".

Okot p'Bitek[4]*:* "Mr President, to put it quite honestly, since the time I was a child, the missions made me sick. I always disliked having to call the Anglican missionaries 'Reverend' and the Catholic priests 'Father'; the Anglicans were not particularly deserving of reverence and the Catholics were not my father. I still get annoyed when I think of how in religious instruction classes we had to sing pious European hymns and repeat things like parrots! No, thank you! Since I studied social anthropology I have lost any respect for the missions I may have had. In the course of this study I have discovered the deep-rooted connections between missionary activity and Western science, and you must understand, Mr President, that we intellectuals can no longer be expected to take the christian Churches seriously . . ."

The President: "Mr Okot p'Bitek, you applied to speak in your own name only; would you, therefore, please leave the other intellectuals out of it".

Okot p'Bitek: "In the autumn of 1960 I began my studies at Oxford. In the very first lecture I heard at the Institute of Anthropology the professor spoke of Africans as if he were speaking of barbarians, savages, primitive people. I protested, but to no effect; the professor knew better. The other professors used the same kind of offensive language. In the library I found a great number of books and magazine articles which used the same expressions. So I wrote a book myself about the African religions as seen through the eyes of Western 'scholars' — 'scholars'

[4] The text is based substantially on Okot p'Bitek's observations in his book *African religions in Western scholarship* (Nairobi 1970).

always, please, in inverted commas! — from the beginning until the present day. The most important fact my investigations brought to light was that these 'scholars' and their followers, no matter how violently they might argue among themselves about questions of method, were united in the conviction that the world's population was divided into two halves, their own — the civilised, and the other — the uncivilised. Now the missionaries — and this is important in this context — were soaked in this pseudo-scholarship and reinforced it by the reports they sent back home, reports which, like the chameleon, changed their colour from one age to another.

"To begin with, for centuries horrific reports about the African peoples were disseminated. It was easy enough to keep people entertained for hours with stories like those which were spread about from the early 16th century until almost the middle of the 20th century. In the 16th century, Duarte Lopez wrote of a 'great number of carved images of demons of varied and terrifying forms. Many people', he said, 'pray to winged dragons, others have as their gods serpents, others rams or tigers or other horrible and loathsome beasts'. O. Dapper, writing in the 17th century, filled a thick volume about Africa with his observations, which he summed up as follows: 'The Kaffirs serve neither God nor idols. They know nothing at all about God but live like animals'. He is able to tell us, further, that the people are lechers, thieves, swindlers, liars and gluttons and that they eat like animals rather than like men! An 18th century traveller put it this way: 'No one, no matter how thorough and careful his investigations, has ever been able to find among all the Kaffirs and Hottentots or coastal dwellers the least trace of religion or of homage paid to God or to the devil'.

"Until quite recently the Churches spoke constantly of the 'heathens, idolaters, men in the shadow of death' and as late as 1965 the Second Vatican Council, in its Decree *On the Church's Missionary Activity* (n. 10), observed with horror that there are still 2,000 million people — and this number is getting bigger every day — who have not heard or have only just heard the Gospel; as if that bothered us! The 'scholars' and the missionaries too have always looked at us through their eyes, through the spectacles of their interests, instead of looking at us as we really were.

"But when at last the Western 'scholars' began to discover in our religion some kind of deity above the spirits, they tried at first to explain this fact by postulating earlier contacts between Negroes and Jews or Christians; after all, the Negroes could hardly have come up with such an idea by themselves! But this explanation didn't tally and so one group of 'scholars' proposed a series of stages of development from the tribal, communal life of men without religion to primitive religious conceptions and, then, by way of manism, totemism and other -isms to monotheism which, in the foreseeable future would, they argued, give way to the scholarly, post-religious man. Another group of 'scholars', the orthodox researchers, who include people like M. Müller, E. Smith and the Africans J.B. Danquah, K.A. Busia and my friend (whose views I do not share) J. Mbiti, are trying hard to explain this African god as a supreme god, indeed to claim that he is the christian God and on this basis to initiate a dialogue. This is no more than a new tactical move in their proselytism, but it marks a welcome change from their earlier arrogance! We Africans are, of course, not convinced by this interpretation because we know nowadays that the many names used for the so-called 'God', such as Mungu, Jok, Nzambi, and so on, referred not to a person but to mysterious, inexplicable forces and natural powers. Basically, then, if one wants to use the term 'religion', what we are talking about is an atheistic religion.

"However, the 'scholars' carried on cheerfully and tried to find a place for this African god in the categories of hellenistic theology. They spoke of an 'eternal', 'omnipresent', 'omnipotent', 'omniscient' god whereas the Africans said simply that god is 'old', 'big', 'strong' and 'wise'. These so-called specialists are nothing but intellectual smugglers; they introduce concepts and structures to Africa which don't belong here. Moreover, they use African religion just as they would use their own mercenaries in order to reach their own goals and to defend their own arguments.

"They have confused the minds of our children in a classroom-religion by talking about 'absolute certainty' and 'eternal principles' and by using the abstract formulas of people like Thomas Aquinas. They have injected into our children a basic attitude of other-worldliness, a notion quite alien to African religion which is explicitly concerned with this world and helps man to control his life more effectively. They have imbued our children with fear and panic in the face of sexuality, whereas we Africans have a very positive attitude to sexuality and accept it from our earliest years.

"This certainty is, of course, being shaken now. Sigmund Freud unmasked religion as an illusion which has no future because man cannot remain for ever a child who, in all the difficulties of life, will place himself trustingly in the hands of his father. Karl Marx for his part declared that we can only reach true happiness if we get rid of religion, which is imagined happiness and must be abolished. And Lenin added that anyone who tries to make a god, is prostituting himself in a disgraceful way because he is concerning himself only with himself and is making gods of his dirtiest, most stupid and most servile instincts.

"Protestant theology has already been shaken more severely than its Catholic counterpart. Beginning with Dietrich Bonhoeffer and going via Rudolf Bultmann to John Robinson a process of thorough demythologisation has taken place, the magical separation between sacred and profane has been abrogated, the supernatural superstructure has been torn down and life as such has been shown to be meaningful. A theology of the death of God has been developed and theologians have quietly admitted that it is probably better to be silent about God than to speak about him.

"If this is what happens to the green wood, what will happen to the dry? If the christian God has been dethroned, how can the African deities survive the scientific and philosophical revolution? Until now the gods have been stopgaps, they have had to jump in to account for everything which man could not control or explain. Nowadays we call this scientific laziness and superstition. The gods have become an intellectual luxury and metaphysical statements about them no longer have any meaning for modern man.

"Mr President, as far as I am concerned then, the missions do not need to be condemned. What is past, is past. Let us leave the dead to bury their dead. We need not bother about the future of the missions; they have no future!"

This line of argument makes quite an impact, but gradually the dumb-founded silence in the lobbies relaxes. Someone points out that in Russia of all places, more than 60 years after the Revolution and enlightenment, there is coming to life, precisely among the young and the intellectuals, a new longing for religion, that professed Marxists are speaking quietly or even aloud of man's eternal homesickness and are declaring that, while God as an old man with a beard is really unacceptable, God as Absolute Future, God as the Transcendent Meaning of History is not irreconcilable with the Marxist world-view. Now if that sort of thing can happen in Russia, then the Africans will certainly not become men without religion all that quickly, if indeed they ever will. Some people believe that a dose of Marxism might even be beneficial to Africa so that the Christians, who in many places have received Baptism far too quickly, will have to learn how to give an honest account of the hope which gives them life.

* * *

After the interval the audience awaits anxiously the speech of Rolf Italiaander. There have been varied and contradictory rumours about him. Some thought that he would produce a spicy dish while others believed that he had been converted to Christianity. But if the latter were the case, why was he going to speak for the prosecution? And so the views are tossed to and fro until he mounts the rostrum.

The President: "You are now going to hear Rolf Italiaander, one of the most travelled and most prolific of writers. He has written over 20 books on Africa. We have reason to be eager to hear what he has to say to us".

Rolf Italiaander[5]*:* "Mr President, to be honest with myself and with you I must confess that not only the missions but I myself have changed in the course of time. In my early days I judged the missions very critically and formulated harsh accusations against them. The missionaries thought, to a great extent, in the same way as the colonialists. They acted as if — well, as if, for instance, the Negroes were our stupid little baby brothers who should be treated like children in a playground. For centuries they, along with other travel-writers, helped to draw and to hawk around the pictures of savages. Jahnheinz Jahn has written a book on this question.

"Now the suckling has taken his revenge on Christianity and on white men as such in that Africans, now that they have achieved their own identity, reject Christianity together with white civilisation. Both Protestant scholars on missionary matters and the headquarters of the Catholic missions, the Roman Congregation for the Evangelisation of Peoples, have recently published reports on the seriousness of the situation. They fear that the missionaries will be characterised as the rear-guard of the imperialistic colonialists and that they will be

[5] The thoughts come from Italiaander's books, *Der ruhelose Kontinent*, pp. 620-624, and *Profile und Perspektiven*, pp. 7ff.

attacked accordingly. On the whole, in the past, to accept Christianity was to accept colonialism and to accept Islam was to join the vanguard of anti-colonialism.

"It used to be said that the colonial authorities did not always send the best men to Africa but rather the black sheep, people who in Europe didn't make much of a go in the army, in commerce or in industry and whom they were keen to get rid of. This was true also, I'm afraid, of some missionaries and the exceptions only proved the rule. Such exceptional people, Fr Placide Tempels for example, often had difficulties with their own superiors. The missionaries did not revolt against the many kinds of racial barriers but even respected them. In many mission-stations one could observe how any disreputable white adventurer could come into the missionary's house through the front door whereas black men, even catechists, had to come in through the back door.

"The American Negro writer Richard Wright in his book about Ghana makes a leading African say: 'I am simply at a loss to imagine what the average missionary was thinking to himself when he was preaching his white Christianity to us. The missionaries knew that if one were to take away a part of our complex make-up, the whole thing would collapse. Their goal must have been, therefore, to break our will to defend ourselves. Where the seed of christian teaching fell, there the will to resist was weakened'. Wright adds: 'The longer I reflected on the work of the missionaries, the stranger it appeared to me. These men, spurred on by neurotic instincts, have destroyed a people's whole philosophy of life without replacing it by another one, indeed without even knowing what they were doing'.

"I used to pass on, uncritically, judgements like this and thus gave my approval to them. Meanwhile, 20 years have gone by and in that time I have continued to travel a lot in Africa and in all the other continents. Whereas previously I had serious misgivings about the traditional work of the missions and preferred to avoid meeting missionaries, I have come to realise that they and their wives (or, in the Catholic missions, the nuns) do very useful work indeed. Often they are the only ones who take responsibility for suffering humanity. The longer I thought over my experiences, the clearer it became to me that, even from the standpoint of a liberal Christian, the bank-balance of the missionaries is in the black.

"In the world of today there is not a single thing which is not called into question. Why, then, should the missionaries be spared a critical examination? In my view, many people of the present time have fallen victim to a deep-seated perplexity and even desperation. They are looking for something and they do not cease to look without knowing what it is they are looking for. There are many more people that one does not see, who are basically looking for God. This is encouraging. For this reason, I believe one should not disrupt the work of the missionaries who, to the best of my knowledge and with a good conscience, were proclaiming God. One should not see only the defects in their work. There you have my accusation and my 'not-guilty' in one go!"

Thursday, May 29

First Vice-President: "Ladies and gentlemen, whether you like it or not, the prosecution continues and our first speaker today is the French author, Jean-Pierre Lycops. In the course of his journeys in Latin America and Africa, Monsieur Lycops has been making a study of the mechanisms of the relationship centre-periphery and in a recent book he has described what he calls 'disguised aggression' and 'cultural genocide' in Africa".

Jean-Pierre Lycops [6]*:* "Mr President, for 13 years I have been studying the psycho-sociological connections between

[6] The account is based on Lycops' book, *Il genocidio culturale* and in particular on the chapter entitled *Divulgare la nozione del peccato per poter salvare*, pp. 19-51.

the poor and the rich countries. In the course of this study I have observed more and more that economic, political and religious power-centres kept the non-Western world in a state of dependence without any problems. This was the first stage. In the second stage these power-centres brought the subject-peoples, by means of the ideological influence they exercised on them, to such a state that the latter identified themselves with the system of subjection. In the present, third stage, the subject countries have indeed achieved freedom; they have the majority of votes in the United Nations and in the Church too, on the plane of theology, they have been awarded their autonomy in finely-worded decrees. But in practice, in concrete terms, the mechanism of suppression and dependence continues — in disguise — just as it did before. A new and worse element has been introduced: the authorities in the countries concerned have become accomplices in their own suppression as well as victims of it. Anyone who has his eyes open and uses them cannot help but cry out. This is what I have done in my book, this is what I am doing on this platform. In the present company I will confine my remarks to the subject of religious aggression.

"In the view of the christian power-centre, man is a sinner, indeed he is born a sinner and has, therefore, to be saved. He is saved already in the first week of his life by means of water and salt. In this way a man is harnessed to the moral system of this society before he is aware of his own identity. The mythology of original sin was constructed to get all men, as sinners, into the snare.

"It is striking that, during the three centuries when the christian peoples were busily engaged in the slave-trade, little was done to christianise Africa. It was only when the Western powers were building up the colonial system that they used the missionaries to give moral support to their venture. All of a sudden the notion of sin was introduced into an environment which until then had been normal and healthy. Morals and customs which were good and right for that society were suddenly pronounced sinful, became immoral and punishable. Anyone who did not give up the traditional ways, became a sinner. For everyone only one remedy was recommended — to fly to the bosom of Holy Mother Church and to the bosom of that society of which she was a part! If one wished to reach paradise, then one had to accept the rules, the morality, the values of this society. This is how the game was won, and under the cloak of ideology, economic exploitation was able to proceed honourably on its way.

"Let's just try to imagine what destructive effects the sudden declaration that polygamy was a sin must have had on the demographic and economic balance of African society. Such a declaration led necessarily to the adoption of Western morality and of the Western economic system, that is, to private ownership, having to think for oneself, egoism, property-hunting, in a word, to capitalism. The importance of Christianity as a theoretical justification for and ideological precursor of colonialism can scarcely be overestimated.

"There are hundreds of examples one could use to illustrate the collapse of tribal life as a result of Christianity, but let us take just one example, the Mossi in Upper Volta. They were an animistic society constantly open to accepting new deities who promised power and prosperity. But the God of the Christians whom they came to accept was unlike the other deities: he did not fit into the social order as they did but claimed a unique and exclusive position. As well as this, he brought with him the colonial system and thereby led this society to its collapse. The French administration realised that the country of the Mossi had little natural wealth; on the other hand, the Mossi themselves could become good labourers in richer and less populated areas. It was no sooner thought of than translated into action. An employment office was set up to attract the Mossi, who left their own country in droves and became cheap and disciplined labour. What were the results of this policy? The Mossi country is today the most christian part of West Africa, but it is also the most impoverished, a terrifying example of economic and cultural impoverishment! The only ones who have remained at home are the women, the children and the elderly. The young people and the men form the proletariat of unskilled workers and unemployed persons from Dahomey to Senegal! It is off-putting to see the bishops of the country from time to time visiting the impoverished villages, collecting money from the inhabitants and in return giving them a blessing and, if time permits, saying Mass.

"In addition to the notion of 'sin', the notion of 'savage' served the same purpose. The missionaries hawked this latter notion around more than anyone else. The more 'savage' a people were whose souls the missionaries were trying to save, the wider the purses of the Christians were opened, the more glorious was the position of the missionaries as heroes in the fight against the lower instincts, against fetishism and cannibalism, and the more justified was the civilising mission of European colonialism. Whereas the notion of 'sinner' included both colonisers and colonised, the notion of 'savage' split the world into two camps and created in the one camp a repulsive superiority complex and in the other a cringing inferiority complex. Topping everything was the doctrine of Noah's curse on the descendants of Cham, that is, the Negroes. These latter accepted their fate piously, suffered because of their colour, envied the non-cursed whites and were grateful not to be entirely rejected by them but to receive at least some help in their need.

"The systematic destruction of the religious and cultural values of Africa had no other purpose than to get the African peoples in one's economic grip. To this end a third notion was employed, that of the 'developed' and 'underdeveloped' countries: 'development' being measured in economic terms. The psychological effect of this notion was the same as that of the other notions, the difference was purely one of words. The 'underdeveloped' peoples suddenly came to regard themselves as poor suckers and the life of the 'developed' peoples was something they dreamt of as a very desirable paradise. Later, the word 'underdeveloped' was tactfully replaced by 'on the road to development' or 'under-industrialised'. But all this juggling with words didn't alter the reality and all these words could have been replaced by 'dependent' countries or 'exploited' countries. From then on, these 'under-peoples' formed an essential part of the developed world, the foundation on which that magnificent building was constructed.

"The image of 'developed' life did not remain merely an abstract notion, it was kept constantly before the eyes of the non-developed peoples. The fine villas of the white men, their splendid cars, rich clothes, good cuisine and the windows of their supermarkets were a constant allurement to the Africans, who carried on slogging away for low wages, and worked even harder at their education that, in the end, they might gain access to that paradise. In this stage use was no longer made of the technique of the inferiority complex; instead, the blacks were allowed to believe that really it wasn't all that difficult to become good and great, clever and rich, like the whites. The missionaries once more played the same tune as the authorities. By means of their impressive churches they led the impoverished faithful to believe the illusion that it was really 'their' church, a pledge, a foreshadowing of the glory that was to be theirs. Using the same methods, the Catholic Church, even in the Middle Ages, had let the people live in poverty and resignation to God's will while the cathedrals abounded in gold.

"But this whole firework display has been extinguished prematurely. The whole of consumer-society is today in a state of economic and psychological bankruptcy. In the so-called 'developed' countries people can be observed rushing in droves to psychiatrists and soothsayers of every kind in the hope of finding a way out of their mental distress and gaining a new inner balance, the loss of which was the price that had to be paid for material prosperity and unrestricted consumption. Gradually people are coming to see, once again, that a man's value depends on what he is rather than what he has, and that the inhabitants of a village in the heart of Africa which has managed more or less to preserve its social structures are much better off than those who have migrated from the villages to the towns in order to seek there access to the wealth of the white man. The former may live in poverty but they do not live in misery, the latter may have more wealth but they are also more wretched!

"Mr President, such are the mechanisms of poverty and exploitation; we cannot pillory them enough and, unfortunately, we can regret them only too late. I accuse the missionaries, however, because they did not see through the trick but allowed themselves to be drawn into it, deliberately or unsuspectingly, and in this way they betrayed their trust. Instead of making the healthy Africans more healthy, they uprooted them, drove them into the jaws of capitalism and handed them over to an internal and external misery from which they can be delivered, not by a miracle, but only by a resurgence of the power of resistance of African man".

* * *

Once again the supporters of the missions leave the hall for the break under a cloud of depression and humiliation. It could certainly be argued that everything has been put in a too one-sided and exaggerated way, that as well as the case of the Mossi there are many other — positive — cases and that the mechanisms of development, the real moving forces of history, are more nuanced than Lycops has presented them. But who is going to make good the shattering effects of his remarks? When will the sun shine again after all this thunder and lightning?

* * *

First Vice-President: "Our second speaker today is a Christian who was persecuted but has survived. His name is Steve Biko and he is a key-figure in the South African Students' Organisation. In 1973 he was placed under house-arrest by the South African government, his writings were not allowed to be printed and his words were not allowed to be quoted in public. Since then the minority government of South Africa has had to slacken the reins; the result is, that we are able to have Steve Biko with us today. Mr Steve Biko, you may speak to us, and you may speak freely".

Steve Biko[7]: "Mr President, at last we black people in Africa have reached the stage where we can speak freely. Until now our voice has been drowned out by the loudspeaker of the white man or else our mouths have been so battered with rubber truncheons that we have been unable to open them. This is because the striving of the white man for power has led him to destroy, brutally and without any consideration, anything and everything which stood in his way. In order to reach their goal and at the same time to preserve a clean image in the eyes of the world, those in power have developed the philosophy of apartheid which, they say, is supposed to be only for our good. But even the most subtle propaganda on the radio and in the press and all the promises in the world about granting freedom to the more developed regions could never convince us that the government was well-disposed towards us; if it were, why did it deprive us of all our human dignity and all our property? Futile police harassment, the ruthless application of that scourge of the people, the pass-laws, the continuing humiliations of every kind were a constant reminder to us Africans that the white man was top-dog and that the black man was only tolerated. It was the white man who was the complete man, and

[7] This speech takes its origin from passages in Biko's essays, *Weisser Rassismus und schwarzes Bewusstsein,* printed in Sundermaier's *Christus, der schwarze Befreier,* pp. 46-61; from other texts in the same book, and from Cone's *Schwarze Theologie.* — Translator's note: Steve Biko died in a South African gaol in September 1977, several months after the original German edition of this book was published.

people of mixed race, Indians and Bantu were lumped together under the heading 'Non-White' as a group of inferior people. This was rubbed into us all the time at the entrance of every post-office, railway station, cinema, bus, public convenience and park. In South Africa there are only white people — and those who aren't! This second group was described by the one essential quality they would always lack — the right skin colour. Their human dignity was not recognised because it was only a white skin that entitled them to full humanity and equal rights. The black man bore, in his own country, at his own place of work, the stamp 'Non'; he went around as a 'Non-being'. You can understand why all this brought us to the point where we could speak of white men only with hatred. This hatred of black men for white men is in no sense pathological, far from it; it is, on the contrary, the sign of a healthy, human reaction to oppression, insults, terrorisation and is a proof that we are not yet completely dead, that we are still able to react.

"Unfortunately, the preaching of the Gospel and the missions were involved in this oppression. The Mau-Mau in Kenya put it succinctly: 'At first, we had the land and the white men had the Gospel. Then the missionaries came and taught us to close our eyes and say our prayers while the white men were stealing our land from us. And now we have the Gospel and they have the land'. In my home in South Africa it was a similar situation. The missionaries, as brothers of the white masters, diverted our attention from this world and its demands and turned it towards a final hope in the future, towards a heaven unconnected with this world. With their moral precepts of humility and obedience they extolled an everlasting life after death. Moreover, the South African State was anchored in Christianity by its constitution. The white missionaries and church-leaders gladly laid claim to all the advantages of the system; they even interpreted colonialism, in whose framework Christianity had a chance of expanding greatly, as salvation-history. The blacks got the impression from the work they did and from the way in which they were instructed that the white man was a kind of god, whose word should never be doubted. Is it surprising that now Christianity is being rejected along with the system to which it belonged?

"You see, in the meantime our hatred has developed into a consciousness of victory. Black consciousness has come alive. It is the most positive cry that ever issued from the black world. It is the realisation that the black men can take part in the game of power-politics as well. We are no longer afraid. The man who is afraid can be overpowered; the man who has no fear cannot be conquered. We are prepared to die on our feet rather than to live on our knees. We regard ourselves now as self-contained beings and no longer as extensions of the white man's broom or lever. Now we know that the true man is beginning to shine forth from the black man.

"We have now reached the stage where we no longer apologise to God for being black but thank him for it. We have now reached the stage where we — Kaffirs, Hottentots, coolies, non-whites — say a loud 'No' to the 'boss', to the 'master', to the white man and so to white racism of every shape and kind, be it that of the tyrant or of the condescending father. We have now reached the stage where we no longer hate white men. Instead, we laugh at them because we know now that it was themselves and not us whom they destroyed by their cynicism; we know now that their politics were nothing other than an attempt by panic-stricken little people to convince one another that they could dominate the blacks for ever and ever; we know now that their paper castles are collapsing. And all of us cry 'Amen' to that!

"We are not, however, so stupid that, in rejecting the Christianity of the white men, we reject Christianity altogether. Rather, we believe we have discovered true Christianity, that is to say, a black theology, a black Christ, a black Church. We black people can see God only with the eyes of black people. Black theology's task, developed by black Fathers of the Church, is to see and interpret the conditions of life of the black man in the light of God's revelation in Jesus Christ, thus creating among black people a new understanding of black dignity. This black theology will give us the courage necessary to unmask white racism and finally inter it. Black theology is not a longing for something in the past, but is an African expression of faith in the future, in our future. Black theology aims to present the essence of christian belief in such a way that we black people can accept it with conviction. Black theology will give us the creative reply to the oppression of black people in the past, it will provide us with a spiritual homeland, the homeland of our new identity. Black theology affirms everything Christ affirmed — humanity, health, joy, freedom; it rejects everything Christ rejected — sickness, hunger, sadness, bondage. Black theology will teach us that God has sent us another Moses to lead us out of Egypt and that God is making his history with us, his people.

"Therefore, in the future we will no longer see the child Jesus and his mother as white people with wavy hair and blue eyes; we will see them as black people with curly hair, thick lips and shining black eyes. Therefore, we will no longer celebrate the Lord's Supper with European bread and wine, we will celebrate it with millet-gruel and palm-wine. Therefore, we will no longer paint the devil black, we will paint him white; we will no longer describe innocence as white, we will describe it as black. All this will come to be, it is already under way, it is already knocking at the door, it is already coming in. Then we will be at home in this black Church and in this black Church every black man will be allowed to say what is on his mind.

"But we charge the white men's Church for being the Church of the white men for us as well as for them, for lacking men of vision, for the fact that we and we alone had to win our freedom and to discover our blackness, for continuing to believe that it had to keep on protecting us and for not having yet come to the introspection and conversion which the black Church demands of it. Until the Church of the white men repents, it remains in the dock".

Friday, May 30

Second Vice-President: "Ladies and gentlemen, it is not only the enemies of the Church who have reservations about the missions and make accusations against them, it is not only those outside the Church who attack it; people within the Church attack it too. Our first speaker today is Fr Kalenga Matembele, a Zairean priest from the parish of Somboshi in Shaba. He is speaking in the name of African Catholic priests from different countries".

Fr Kalenga Matembele [8]*:* "Mr President, we do not wish to split the Church into a white Church and a black Church. We are working for unity, but unity in plurality and it is precisely for this reason that we have to hold up to ridicule many of the things which the missionaries have put forward as being alone right and which no one has questioned until now. In doing this, we are in no sense overlooking the great degree of dedication shown by the missionaries and the positive results of their work. Even the most prejudiced of people, provided they retain a little in the way of objectivity, recognise that the rise of Africa and its entry into the circle of modern nations is due largely to the missionaries; even our critical thinking in their regard is the fruit of their activity.

"But there had to be a reaction against a particular kind of missionary activity and this reaction goes back as far as 1956. In that year, for the first time and to the great surprise of the missionaries, 13 black priests spoke up and asked questions. This denoted a change in the self-aware-

[8] This speech summarises thoughts expressed by some African priests, including Fr Matembele, in the magazine *Spiritus*, no. 56 (Paris 1974) and which other African priests had already given vent to in 1956 in *Des prêtres noirs s'interrogent* by V.A.

ness of the black priests. Until then the missionaries had been the Church's loudspeakers. They dealt with and resolved our problems — for us, without us and, often, against us. We were the Church of silence. But at last we found the courage to discover ourselves, to ask about our identity, to put ourselves forward in the Church as partners who were to be taken seriously. The first congress of black artists and writers in Paris in 1956 strengthened our hand in this matter. This congress marked the revelation of black culture. After such a long period of humiliation Africa has become a personality with a normally developed self-awareness instead of continuing to endure for ever the superiority complex of white men and to suffer from its own inferiority complex.

"In this matter all we have done is to take the documents of the Church seriously; on a theoretical level, these documents have allowed us the position we have adopted but, in practice, with regard to many missionaries in the past and even in the present, things are very different. This is why we must now, as then, speak out and accuse the missions.

"The real 'implantation of the Church' has not yet taken place in Africa. We are not yet a 'local' Church, but merely a faded copy of the European Church. The missionaries have given us not the Bible but the *Summa theologica*. In their schools we have become mini-Europeans, cold, bloodless intellectuals instead of mystics. African religion was primarily life, power, centre and meaning of life; now we have ended up in a net of commands and laws. Whereas Yahweh revealed himself as the God of the history of his people, we have had to take over fossilised forms and formulas from the history of another people. The missionaries could not distinguish between what was suitable for export and what wasn't and they blindly brought us the whole burden of their customs, their laws, their rites, their priestly caste instead of new life and new hope.

"But now the reaction is under way. We are living

in the age of Incarnation-theology. Now that Africa has been christianised, Christianity must be africanised. Thank God, we are being helped in this attempt by different governments and heads of state, who are talking about 'negritude', authenticity and returning-to-ourselves. These words are not directed against Christianity as such, but they are directed against the spiritual alienation and cultural uprooting which the missions have brought us.

"But, as has usually been the case in the course of history, the Church as an institution has failed to realise the meaning of these reactions; it has seen its structures threatened and has spoken of the persecution of Christians. It is unwilling to admit that it has been concerning itself too much with ecclesiastical centralism, which it should at last have been demolishing. In reality, the missions were not so much concerned to bring the Good News to another people as to expand among that people the Church in its European-Roman form. The African in himself was of no 'interest'; he was of interest only in so far as he entered the Church and heartily joined in its work. Anyone who did not conform to the mould made by the missionaries was excluded from entry through any doorway in heaven or on earth. Thus, a young person who did not conform had no chance of receiving higher education, a worker who did not conform had no hope of being employed in the missions and a sick person who did not conform was not certain of being treated with the same care as others. The rule was: 'Everything or nothing'. The choice was between accepting Christianity as a whole just as it was presented or receiving nothing. Everything had to proceed according to the imported pattern and in no other way. For instance, if a person used African medicinal herbs or took part in African dances or festivals, he was punished on the grounds that all these things came from the devil. Anyone who didn't toe the party-line exactly put his career in jeopardy. The missionaries, instead of building bridges between the cultures and feeding the Church with the richness of

Africa, tried to make us obedient courtiers of the Roman Church.

"A problem of a unique kind is priestly celibacy. We are in no way denying the value and witness of remaining unmarried for the sake of the kingdom of heaven, but we quite fail to understand how this free offer, this invitation, can be made into an obligation for all who wish to serve the Church as priests — and this in a country like Africa, where marriage occupies such a central position in life. Before the Synod of Bishops in 1971, 83 per cent of the 595 African priests in Zaire spoke out in favour of making celibacy optional, but the Synod went against this large majority. Our views were asked, but they were not listened to. Thus a split arose between priests and bishops, between the African and the European Church.

"Partly because of the law of celibacy we have just as serious a disproportion between white missionaries and African priests as we had before. On average, we African priests make up only one third of the priests in Africa. We feel stifled by the overwhelming presence of the missionaries. We are still a colony of the Church. The independent states were able to get rid of many white men, keeping only those they needed and wished to keep. In the Catholic Church this process has not yet taken place. The Church is the only organisation in Africa which is still dominated with regard to personnel, money and ideas by the West. In no sense do we want to lapse into enmity towards foreigners — this would be a new kind of racism, but the missionaries, who come to spend the rest of their lives among us and take up residence in our countries like colonists, like foreign settlers, simply contribute to the fact that we remain for ever a 'missionary country' and they prevent the breakthrough of African vocations and of a truly African Church. In spite of everything they continue to behave like lords of the missions, like teachers who want to bring us civilisation, technology and religion. We cannot rid ourselves of the impression that they enjoy being in this situation and that this is why they have no wish to return to Europe. We haven't all that much faith in their devotion and unselfishness in the spirit of the Gospel.

"In the Protestant Churches the idea of a moratorium was seriously discussed at the Assemblies in Bangkok (1973) and Lusaka (1974). John Gatu, Secretary General of the Presbyterian Church of East Africa, was one of the speakers who expressed his views on this point very clearly. He said: 'Our present problems can be solved only if all missionaries leave the country so as to give both sides a period of at least five years in which to think over and formulate anew their relationships for the future. The Church of the Third World must be given the possibility of finding its own identity, but the powerful presence of the missionaries is an obstacle to this self-finding of the Churches'.

"The Roman decrees and the declaration of the African bishops after the 1974 Synod speak of the local Churches and say that missionaries should fit themselves into them in a subordinate role. But, we ask, are the missionaries really capable of such an adaptation? Most of them probably aren't. They are a product of their race which is distinguished by its unpleasant habit of being always a giver and never a receiver. Thus, even the most well-intentioned missionaries will have difficulties in making the adaptation demanded of them. Without being aware of it, they are constantly contradicting themselves. They talk about wanting to respect the African personality, wanting to give free rein to the African Church. But as soon as it is a question of concrete matters touching their interests or convictions, they forget their principles and with all the toughness of their race they defend their title of master and throw their opponents out of the ring. Now the average African, convinced as he is of the superiority of his opponent, retires into his shell and swallows the bitter, humiliating fact that he still has to hold his tongue even in matters affecting the core of his personality. This is why many, even among educated Africans, say in a tone of resignation: 'We can do nothing. As long as the missionaries are in our country, we will never be able to achieve our own identity'. Mr President, if you and your elders know a way out of this uneasy situation, we will be grateful to hear it".

* * *

Second Vice-President: "The uneasiness mentioned by the previous speaker is clearly not something felt only by a few hot-heads. This being so, we are going to allow a second speaker to talk on the same topic. Fr Meinrad P. Hegba, a Jesuit from the Cameroons, is a professor at the 'Institut Supérieur de Culture Religieuse' in Abidjan and at the Gregorian University in Rome. Fr Hegba has made a name for himself by his many articles and lectures and by his recent book on the emancipation of the protected Churches".

Fr Meinrad P. Hegba[9]*:* "Mr President, some critics, while accepting the ideas underlying my book, have reproached me with having written it in a harsh and embittered tone. To this I reply without hesitation: In Africa the time for writing gallant, soothing books is past. If a solution isn't found in good time, every crisis, every conflict reaches its climax and when that happens, people must no longer talk, they must cry out so that even those who are not aware of the conflict will notice what hour has struck. Fr Kalenga Matembele has portrayed the problems of Zaire; I would like to confirm and fill out his observations in order to show that these problems are to be found in other countries too.

"When I talk about the emancipation of the protected Church, it is perhaps good to situate this in a wider con-

[9] The account is based substantially on Hegba's book, mainly on pp. 148-169, and on thoughts expressed when it was launched in Rome on February 28, 1977.

text. For the last 25 years the whole of the Third World has been engaged in a comprehensive process of emancipation. This process began with the Conference of Bandung in 1955, the signal for political emancipation. This was followed in 1956 by the first congress of black artists and writers in Paris, the signal for cultural emancipation. The meeting of religions in Kyoto, Japan, in 1970 was the signal for religious emancipation and the economic conference of the Afro-Asiatic countries in Algiers in 1973 together with the oil crisis shortly afterwards was the signal for economic emancipation. The 1974 Synod of Bishops in Rome gave the signal for ecclesiastical emancipation always, of course, within the framework of the one universal Church. Unfortunately, however, the demands made at this Synod by the bishops of the Third World regarding the authenticity, the africanisation and the incarnational character of the Gospel — demands which were subsequently agreed to in the Apostolic Exhortation *Evangelii Nuntiandi* — are simply being ignored in practice and in concrete legislation. Unfortunately, too, our African bishops haven't the courage necessary to press their point, nor to protest relentlessly against the continuance of a patronising attitude, nor to speak in Africa as they spoke in Rome and then simply to go their own way.

"The only foundation on which we must build is Christ and his Gospel, not the whole christian ethos of 2,000 years of Western history, Western theology, spirituality and ecclesiastical discipline. Jesus Christ nowhere said that the only right Africans had was to add a little folklore to the Roman liturgy for fear that they might otherwise depart from the orthodox faith. The Churches of Africa must demand a lot of freedom in the liturgy and in other areas unless they want to remain for all time no more than an off-print of the Western Church. We Africans do not wish to compose Eucharistic Prayers in accordance with our own tastes and our own faith and to impose them on the whole Church, and we do not wish that the same thing should be done to us. As long as it is being done, it only proves that Europe is still dominating us and colonising us, this time using religion as a cover-up.

"This is why we speak out very clearly and say: However marvellous Western or Eastern Christianity may be, we want to build upon Christ and not upon a Western interpretation of his message. We respect the saints, the artists, the theologians, the canon lawyers and the luminaries of whom Europe and America are proud in a spirit of christian humility. But we want to be ourselves. We no longer wish to be mere commentators on and faithful imitators of these great souls. We have to create an original, truly African theology. Of course we will make mistakes and even succumb to errors, but these won't be any worse than those to be found in the history of East and West. Let those Churches of Europe and America which are without fault cast the first stone at us. I am not recommending that we reject the first-rate tools for work provided by Western literature; all I am saying is that, in future, we must use them with a certain freedom of spirit and no longer have the almost superstitious reverence for them which has made us perpetual students and imitators. To gain a true estimate of their value, we perhaps need a period of time during which we will renounce them completely and cut ourselves off from them. Until now, the intellectual and spiritual freedom we have had has been only that of a bird in a cage or of a tourist on a package-holiday. We haven't had the least bit of elementary, evangelical freedom.

"Regarding the missionaries, it must be said that, of late, they have tried to behave differently from their predecessors; we will not go into the question of whether they have done so out of honesty or as a matter of tactics. But basically these ambassadors of Christ and of the West have not altered. Most of them no longer have the nerve to kick people or to box their ears for not paying their church dues, or to tear off their headscarves and jewellery, but their arrogance, covered with a thin layer of good-naturedness, suddenly breaks through again whenever they are placed without warning into the right situation. It has never been our experience that missionaries have flared up against or assaulted white men, who are not always model Christians. But this is how they have reacted in the past — and how they sometimes still react — towards black men. What is more tragic still is that, when something like this happens, all the missionaries stick together and defend the behaviour of their colleague. This is why we cannot avoid saying that the majority of missionaries are, and always will be, incurably white and foreign.

"To sum up, what we wish for is a long moratorium in which we will be left alone with our God, so that his Spirit can visit us — without intermediaries and witnesses, without having to request permission from some distant authority, so that his light can enlighten us without having, as it did until now, to pass through the prism of a foreign culture.

"The so-called 'militants', the aggressive activists of Catholic Action in France, the Young Catholic Workers, the Young Catholic Students and the Young Catholic Farmers, do not come off any better. They come from the West, where their movements have failed, to see if they can succeed in Africa. They get involved in practices which in no way correspond to the Gospel, they criticise the religious and the civil authorities, they arouse public opinion against this or that African priest or pastor whom they regard as anti-French to such a point that the poor victim is banished from his own diocese and his own country. Such is the power, the almost unlimited power, these foreigners have.

"Spirits like this cannot be driven out by prayer and fasting alone; more vigorous measures are needed. Such cancerous members must be cut off and the building-up of our Church continue with the remaining genuinely apostolic workers. Only in this way can the Church grow up healthy and viable. Those missionaries who are really working together with us and who no longer always make common cause with their brethren for reasons of racial or national solidarity may continue, in subordinate positions, their apostolate among us, but they should no longer hold any key positions or have anything to do with politics or financial administration.

"We know that Christianity in itself is an Eastern religion but that it was taken up by the West which, having stamped it with the indelible seal of its philosophy, its law and its culture, offered it in this form to the other peoples of the world. Today we want to impress our seal upon Christianity for Africa, we want to make it at home in our world of ideas without at the same time holding up our impress as divine revelation, which is what happened in the case of aristotelean-thomistic philosophy, the German Protestant and Anglican Reformations and the usages of France, Portugal and other countries. We want to have at last 'our' Church, an African 'local Church' in which we can feel at home and with which we will be on as good terms as we are with ourselves.

"The paternalistic type of missions is at long last over and done with; it must die, so that a truly African Christian Church can arise. What of the protective type of missions which lives on in satellite Churches, in quasi-Churches which never have and never will reach their majority? May it rest in peace! And what of the divine and apostolic mission of sister-Churches, which with dignity practise community and mutual dialogue? Long may they live! Mr President, I have nothing to add to this except to say: Let us go forward and act!"

* * *

Second Vice-President: "On our agenda for today we have a third speech. Our speaker now is Horst Müller, who was born in 1959 and is a student at the Teachers' Training College in Augsburg, Germany. It will certainly be interesting to hear the views of a young Christian from one of the old evangelising countries on Operation Missions".

Horst Müller[10]: "My generation has, in a manner of speaking, fallen down from heaven to earth, from romanticism to reality; it has made a breakthrough from mythology to history. When we were ten years of age, we felt the same enthusiasm for the heroic missionaries as we did for Robinson Crusoe and Old Shatterhand. Since that time our eyes have been opened and we have found out what the missions are like; we now accuse them.

"As we see it, the whole missionary enterprise arose, historically speaking, from the arrogant superiority of Europeans linked with their intolerance and their striving for power in the Church. It was a question of extending the Church's sphere of influence, winning prestige, drawing — with the help of the annual publication of numbers of converts — a triumphalistic picture and basking in the awareness of being the largest religious group in the world. As long as Europe had political and economic mastery over the rest of the world, it was easy to make out as *the* religion of the world. Since then Europe has become a part of the world and has to manoeuvre very carefully so as not to be pushed off the edge. In the same measure Christianity has become one religion among many and now, at long last, must bury all its ideas of superiority and claims to absolutism. Only by cutting back and taking a more modest attitude has it a chance of saving what can be saved.

"The same lack of tolerance shown towards other religions operated also in the not very edifying rivalry among the missionary institutions. Instead of regarding themselves as servants of the one cause of Christ, they rose up against each other, took parishes from each other, fought over the boys and girls whom they hoped to make into missionaries and nuns and tried to get together as much money as possible for their own missions. This conflict continued in the missionary magazines with each

[10] Horst Müller is an imaginary character. The ideas attributed to him could have been gleaned from conversations with young people not many years ago.

group wanting every family to buy its own magazine. Hence a great number of non-profit-making magazines was produced; these were so uninspired in design and content as to attract the interest only of uncritical children and of elderly people who were thinking of heaven and wanted to do some more good deeds before they died. To impress naïve and sentimental people like this, the magazines depicted, in a dozen different ways, the outstretched hands of sick, leprous, deformed or starving beggars. Finally, those who, by putting some coins in the box, made the figure of a black child on the box nod his head, or even went so far as to send silver paper and used stamps to the missions, could have an easy conscience in the conviction that for a week at least they had prevented want in Africa! Now all this hasn't really helped the Africans to escape from their want; they have been left as beggars instead of being given constructive economic help to build themselves up. They were portrayed to us as idolaters and savages when the convincing power of their culture ought to have been shown to us. In this way both we and they were deluded and made fools of — as long as we allowed ourselves to be made fools of.

"Then there was all this talk about saving souls, this unenlightened theology of soul-saving which for centuries filled the missionaries with a fanatical zeal we nowadays find almost unbelievable. Let's leave the saving of souls to God, he has a hundred ways of saving them if he wants to. He doesn't need us to save souls, he needs us to save men. Our most urgent concern is not souls but men, not heaven but earth, not treatises but tractors, not bibles but bread. If Pope Paul VI could write in *Populorum Progressio*, 'The new word for peace is development', then we could logically say, 'The new word for missions is development'. But here as elsewhere it is a long way from theory to practice. Still too many of the Church's prelates are frightened of what is called horizontalism and humanisation; they talk of verticalism and evangelisation. In this way they split man up and present him with a choice of alternatives rather than with a synthesis which alone would stand a chance of being accepted and taken seriously.

"It suffices to look at the fruits of such a conception of the missions. Rigid legalism, abstract dogmatism have been imported, the heads of children and catechumens have been filled with formulas and they have been indoctrinated with those virtues leading only to the saving of their souls. And thus the pupils of the mission-schools have become pious egoists, inhibited people, ruthless go-getters who, once their country achieved independence, quickly formed the class of the *nouveaux riches* and thought more of themselves than of the ordinary people.

"What is needed today is not an isolated religion which alone has a hot line to heaven but an integrated religion, consisting of contact with the world, the furthering of human values and an autonomous morality which guarantees to man and to the human community the greatest possible self-development. If then from all this there *also* comes up the question about an ultimate meaning of life and a religious answer appears to be appropriate, so much the better. But for the moment, man as man has priority. In this regard, the missions as they have always been understood must either adapt their views accordingly or pack up!"

Saturday, May 31

The President: "Ladies and gentlemen, as you know, Africa — even when it had no written literature — was never without literature; it had its walking libraries, its troubadours, its wise men. But nowadays Africa has an abundance of native writers who express the thoughts and feelings of their own people. Today we are going to hear one of the leading writers, Beti Mongo, a Catholic from the Cameroons. He is going to give us his views of the missions. Beti Mongo has made a name for himself with his book *Le pauvre Christ du Bomba* and other novels".

Beti Mongo [11]: "Mr President, I have come here, not to attack the missions, but simply to point to certain things which I and other writers have noticed. Moreover, we have a certain sympathy with the missions. We owe them a debt of gratitude for their dedication and their work, but at the same time they leave us disillusioned. Now when writers think and write along these lines, they must be taken seriously. Their views carry weight. They are listening devices and they sense what the people are thinking. At the same time they are the loudspeakers of the people. They form the meeting point of ideas and they not only describe the mental climate of Africa but they influence and determine it as well. Their words have more power than those of the priest in the pulpit. It is no coincidence that many writers are politicians — words give one power over people.

"The relationship between the writers and the missions seems to have got off to a good start. The first quarter of this century saw, especially in South Africa, what was called the golden age of African literature; there was a number of classical writers, all of them Christians who shared a tendency towards idealising and moralising. They regarded tribal life and Christianity as an ideological unity. There is hardly a trace of real criticism of the missions to be found in their writings. That age was the age of first love and of childlike trust. They saw only the positive sides of their European teachers whom they worshipped without reserve. But when the economic, social and political shockwaves swept across the country, this stream of books dried up. Nowadays people refer to this kind of literature with a contemptuous smile as 'nursery literature'. This period was followed by one of pronounced drought which lasted until after the Second World War when the climate, one of dawning freedom, became more conducive to literary inspiration.

[11] The account is taken almost verbatim from Beti's novel and from the summary judgement of neo-African literature in S. Hertlein's *Christentum und Mission*, especially pp. 64ff and 111-116.

"This new literature, mainly the work of former pupils of the missions, is of a different nature. In my novel *La pauvre Christ du Bomba* I have described in the form of a diary a two-week safari as seen through the eyes of a loyal houseboy in a Catholic mission-station. The principal character is Reverend Father Superior Drumont, a lean man with a beard and a long robe. A fine, honest priest, deeply convinced of his religious mission as a herald of the Gospel, he has been in the country for 20 years. The children call him simply 'Jesus Christ' and the houseboy says this isn't blasphemy because the good Father deserves the name. Fr Drumont, because of his great zeal for souls, has never, in all the years he has been on the missions, allowed himself the pleasure of going out hunting — all he hunts are souls. Without the assistance of a lay-brother he has built the house for the Fathers, the school and the most beautiful church for miles around. This zeal for building which astounds everyone, even the pagans, has, however, a negative side to it. Church taxes and constant compulsory labour for the building-up of the mission-station led men to the opinion that their priest was no better than a Greek merchant or a colonialist. 'All you people are after', they say, 'is money'. The houseboy denies this and says that all the Father is after is the salvation of his Christians and the advancement of the work of the mission. On the other hand, Fr Drumont speaks the language of the tribe so badly that it takes a whole night's reflection to work out what he has been saying. In his dealings with the black people, even though he is sympathetic towards them and protects them, to the best of his ability, from exploitation by the colonial authorities, he is not exactly gentle. He is hasty, headstrong and unwilling to listen to objections; without a second thought he calls grown women idiots and has them thrashed when they make mistakes. In religious matters in particular he is fanatical and shows little discretion. On the First Friday of the month, in a rage he smashes the dance drums of the pagans and on a Sunday he drags the witch-doctor bodily from his hut and forces him to abjure his superstitions before the altar in the presence of the assembled community. The pagans do not recognise his authority as a messenger of God; to them he is just a white man and they object indignantly: 'Have you ever ranted against the white men who live in the town with bad women?'

"Experiences like this coupled with the uprightness of his character in the end plunge Fr Drumont into a grave inner crisis. He loses confidence in his vocation as a missionary. He has to recognise that Africans in their world are simply not in a position to live according to the christian moral law, that, moreover, missionary work in Africa is impossible if the missionaries cooperate with the European colonial power to the detriment of the black people. This goes against his conscience and so, finally, Fr Drumont leaves his work in the missions and returns to France. It had become clear to him that the white missionary was not made for Africa. The houseboy he has left behind laments: 'Father Superior is gone and we'll certainly never see him again. But why should he come back? We had as little love for him as if he had never been one of us . . . because he was not one of us'. So the novel ends and there is very much more that one could read between the lines.

"In the novel I have taken pains to show both the good and the bad sides of the missionaries. Other authors see primarily the negative aspects and become harsh in the charges they make; this could be proved from any number of novels. An expert like Jahnheinz Jahn is right when he says by way of summary: 'Looking back over the past half century of modern African literature we can say that it began by rejecting African tradition and emphasising Christianity, then it turned more and more away from Christianity and came back to African ways of thought'.

"Now if one draws out the implications of this assessment, an unusual paradox becomes apparent. It is this. The most important black writers turn their attention to religious and christian questions. They clearly have an inner personal need to thrash out such questions. They are lost in admiration for and sympathy with the person of Jesus Christ and the idea of christian brotherly love. But at the same time they reject decisively the concrete forms of Christianity. They regard the Church as an organisation rather than as a body pulsating with holiness. Christian teaching and christian worship are for them closed and incomprehensible areas. The dynamism of the Sermon on the Mount is in harsh contrast to the brutality and day-to-day godlessness of the white Christians. The missionaries and priests are, in their eyes, officials and soulless performers of ritual actions or straitlaced schoolmasters rather than proclaimers of a divine message and mediators of divine life. The work of the missions, since it is so closely linked with European imperialism and cultural superiority, is looked upon as dangerous to African culture. Misuse of spiritual power has shattered the basis of confidence between the missions and the Africans and often leads the latter to turn their backs on Christianity. Most writers received their early formation at mission-schools where they came into close contact with Christianity. The effect of looking back on this period of their lives is not a very flattering one as far as the missions are concerned. In their writings — and usually in their lives too — these writers turned their back on the Church. They turned away from a Christianity which neither met their needs nor fulfilled their longings. In their writings those who have remained true to Christianity are portrayed as naïve and ineffectual, uncritical and ignorant of the world and they are not regarded as being capable of laying a firm grasp on reality. The only hope lies in a few exceptional figures such as native preachers and, for that matter, selfless missionaries; above all, it lies in kindly and understanding teachers. The strength of people like these is not so much Christianity as the fact that they are, first of all, completely men — honest, upright, kindly men — and it is as men that they are at home among the Africans.

In this way, then, they can become credible also as people who lead others to God.

"Mr President, let me repeat: I am not attacking the missions, I am only stating facts and I regret that the image of the missions is, on average, so unpromising. But herein lies a challenge to reply and to reflect. I believe also that the missionaries having, with the departure of the colonial masters, lost their own 'mastery', have changed — indeed had to change. But the golden age of the missions is past anyway and, with few exceptions, the writers of today pay no attention to them whatsoever. This silence itself tells us something too".

* * *

The President: "The last speaker on our list is Harris W. Mobley, a Protestant missionary from Ghana. He will not open the defence but will conclude the case for the prosecution. Mr Mobley".

Harris W. Mobley [12]*:* "Mr President, like the previous speaker, I do not represent the prosecution but rather those who have their eyes and ears open and are honest enough to say what they have seen and heard. Until the present time we have written the history of the missions and even the history of the colonies from our point of view. We have written of our bold enterprises, our great achievements and the good we have done for others. Now we must let these others speak and must learn how they, from their point of view, saw and judged our enterprises and our achievements. Only the two points of view together give the true picture.

"I have spent the best years of my life in Ghana where, in addition to my ordinary missionary work, I have made a study of old church magazines, newspapers and books.

[12] The speech is based on Mobley's book, *The Ghanaian image of the missionary.*

I was very surprised to discover that the Christians of Ghana have been criticising the missionaries openly and vehemently since the beginning of this century. When I studied the matter more closely, it became clear to me how wrong the widespread opinion is that such criticism of the missions was only the fruit of the fanatical nationalism of the post-war era. On the contrary, the criticism in the earlier period was more searching than later criticism, which is why the earlier period came to be spoken of as the 'golden age of criticism'. This criticism, moreover, came from the leaders in Church and State and was understood and approved of by ordinary, illiterate churchgoers; it was regarded as an expression of christian responsibility.

"In other words, the 'good Negroes' had always had much keener vision than we thought. We have to look at ourselves in this reflection and find out who we are. For this reason I believed I would do the mission a service by publishing these criticisms made over seven decades. My Catholic friends tell me that these opinions collected in Protestant circles could be applied, with certain differences, to the Catholic missions. Let us, then, have a look at how our missionary presence was judged by the Africans.

"The first point concerns our typical mission-stations. These were large buildings usually situated on a hill and therefore isolated. That they were built like this in the 19th century as a protection against mosquitoes is understandable, but this pattern continued long after means of preventing malaria and yellow-fever had been found and it then became the pattern for the native clergy also. In this way the 'man of God' set up a barrier between himself and his people not only by his standard of living but also in purely geographical terms. The mission-station got the name 'white man's town'. Even when the missionaries spent a lot of time during the day among the people, this did not remove the fundamental separation and Christianity was increasingly regarded as a religion of foreigners. This became particularly the case when those black Christians who followed the missionaries built their dwellings around the mission-stations. In doing so they withdrew themselves from the authority of the chiefs, indeed they undermined it, and they looked down their noses at their 'pagan' fellow-countrymen and their customs. The Muslim missionaries or, for that matter, the Lebanese and Indian merchants, behaved quite differently. They made their homes right among the people; they lived out the brotherhood of all men whereas the missionaries preached about it but practised the opposite in their daily lives.

"This effective separation of the races was one of the most compelling reasons why, in the case of the Protestant missions, independent African Churches were founded at a quite early stage. The Africans wanted to feel at home; they wanted their Churches to be bone from African bone, flesh from African flesh, just as Christ was completely a member of his own people. How would things have been if Christ had grown up in an African village instead of in Nazareth? The missionaries had none of this intimate closeness to the people. They took their recreation sitting in comfortable chairs with a glass of whisky and a box of cigars at their side. And if, during their recreation period, an African looking for help or a beggar came to them, they found, without any qualms of conscience, a hundred excuses for not doing anything about it. In other ways too they treated black Christian workers harshly. Dr J.K. Aggrey, one of the first men from the Gold Coast to achieve world-wide renown, once said: 'Certain white people ought for once to be changed into Negroes for a few days in order to experience what we experience'. He concluded from this that, for heaven's sake, the Church in Africa should be given African leaders as soon as possible. While saying this, one admits, naturally, that there were missionaries whose daily lives did conform to the doctrine of christian brotherly love and, as a result, they will for ever be remembered in the community.

"But in general the missionaries, in the judgement

of the African Christians, were not servants after Christ's example and demands, but masters. The people suffered under the burden of the white men who regarded themselves as the sole guiding principle of good. The Greeks used to call all who were not Greeks 'barbarians'; similarly the white men regarded the Africans as pagans, a term which connoted night and blindness, error and idolatry, cruelty and immorality. They did not try to see good and bad on both sides and to attribute good thoughts and words to the Africans also. Dr Aggrey expressed this in an apposite comparison when he said that if, when playing the piano, you use either only the white or only the black keys, the result is very impoverished; in order to achieve complete harmony you have to use both kinds of keys. This is how black men and white men ought to complement one another. He comforted his humiliated people by saying: 'My African people, we have been made in the image of God, but we have been taught to think of ourselves as chickens and that is how we really do think of ourselves. But we are eagles, so let's spread our wings and fly'. The white people, including the missionaries, didn't look at it in this way, however; they continued to regard the Negroes as primitive people and to treat them in a paternalistic way. It was only after the War, under the pressure of the movement towards nationhood and in states which had achieved total independence, that the missionaries had to adapt, had to take us seriously, even though their frequently hurtful criticism of us has not ceased in private.

"One main reason for this attitude on the part of the missionaries was that they had been insufficiently prepared for their work. They learned the language of the people very inadequately and, above all, they were not familiar with African customs. They condemned *en bloc* things of which they had no knowledge. In their view they were the teachers of the world and they hadn't the courage to see the whole picture and learn from it. They built christian teaching in the clouds instead of on the firm ground on which the catechumens were standing. The latter, therefore, accepted the new teaching only into their memories and not into their lives. Instead of asking for hospitality from the African religions, Christianity in its arrogance has driven the inhabitants out of their own house and the missionaries, like iconoclasts, have smashed the African religions to pieces. This injustice must be remedied; the missionaries ought to ask pardon, in a public memorial service honouring the dead, of all those they previously despised.

"Of course a reconciliation between Christianity and African culture is very difficult. The African community has already been broken up by misunderstood christian individualism, African marriage has been shaken by the rigid christian laws, African piety — which is expressed in dancing and drum-playing — has been replaced by European hymns and abstract prayers. Philip Gbeho had been trying for years to get the missionaries to introduce African dancing into the christian liturgy, but he was unsuccessful and he declared: 'If we dance, we are excluded from the Church which the missionaries brought us. My parents were, as far as I'm concerned, the most religious people I have ever known. They taught me the Ten Commandments before I had ever seen a white man. They told me dancing is good. The Church then said it is bad. We just don't know what to think! We dance for joy, for sorrow, out of anger and out of piety: for us, dancing is a form of art, a way of self-expression'. The Church has not realised the chance it had.

"Other complaints are voiced too: rivalry between the Churches, misuses of the schools to further the missions, the opposition of the missionaries to national aspirations, and so on.

"Mr President, I cannot take all these statements lightly even though, as a member of a missionary group, I am one of the accused. Clearly, to be just, the other side of the coin would have to be shown; this is soon going to be done by other speakers. However, I would like to add just one thing to Philip Gbeho's melancholy observations; it is this. I would like to recommend you, Mr President, and your council to attend an up-to-date christian service in Ghana or in any other African country. You would then see for yourselves that the African Church is not really so un-African. But I admit that we are still only in the process, not just of translating the Gospel into the African languages, but of implanting it into the African cultures. The future has some surprises in store for us".

The President: "So, ladies and gentlemen, the prosecution has concluded its case. Speaking personally, I must confess that I have been very impressed, indeed shaken. As a non-Christian, I have seen the missions more from the outside, in their greatness, in their achievements. Now I have learned, not for the first time, that if, in dealing with one man or with a group of men, you look below the surface, you see things you would prefer not to have seen. We must take very seriously the statements we have heard, but we mustn't absolutise them and see them in isolation. Next week we will hear the other side of the missions; only after this will it be possible to formulate a balanced judgement and the consequences to be drawn from it. One thing I can state even at this stage: we members of the council of elders are glad that we have withheld from the press so far the not-incorrect but nevertheless one-sided view of things we have heard. From four o'clock this afternoon all the speeches for the prosecution can be obtained from the press-centre and may be disseminated in a balanced way as from Monday. Ladies and gentlemen, I wish you all a pleasant Sunday".

The Case for the DEFENCE

Monday, June 2

The President: "Ladies and gentlemen, the Romans — so I've been told — had a saying which ran, *audiatur et altera pars* ('let the other side be heard also'). They were not alone in this, for every good judicial system including the African one has had the practice of listening to both sides. And so now the missions have the chance to speak in their own defence. The first speaker is Bishop Joseph Blomjous, a Dutch White Father. He was Bishop of Mwanza in Tanzania and during the Second Vatican Council he played an important role in getting the African bishops to talk to each other and come closer to each other. While still relatively young and in full vigour he asked, in 1965, permission to resign his post because he had realised that the leadership of the Church in Africa should, from now on, be left to Africans. Since that time he has been publicising his new ideas and interpretations of events in numerous lectures and articles".

Bishop Joseph Blomjous[13]: "Mr President, even after being under fire for many days, the missions will not admit defeat. I am standing here before you, an elderly bishop, laden, as it were, with all the complaints made

13 The thoughts are taken for the most part from Hertlein's *Wege christlicher Verkündigung*, vol. I, pp. 12-107; they have been examined and approved by Bishop Blomjous.

against the missionaries — but I still hold my head high. I do not intend to refute the charges made, nor do I intend to lay before you the good the missionaries have done — that will be the task of later speakers; all I want to do is to help you understand the not-so-good things the missionaries did and to suggest extenuating reasons for them by putting all the charges that have been made into their proper setting.

"Firstly, I want to speak of the psychological setting. None of us lives an abstract human life in a vacuum. We all were, and we remain always, children of our time. True enough, one can in retrospect judge the attitudes of earlier generations but one cannot simply condemn them without more ado. One cannot blame any Christian for not thinking before the Second Vatican Council and before the World Conference of the World Council of Churches at Uppsala in the same way that people began to think and to act after these events. Similarly, it would be just as wrong to blame the Churches for the fact that Vatican II did not take place until the early sixties and the Uppsala meeting until 1968 as it would be to blame anyone for the fact that, 50 years ago, penicillin was unknown and that jet-travel and TV-satellites were not being used for communications.

"Looked at from today's viewpoint, we can consider many of the things done in the past as being no longer right even when we leave out of account the real defects and human weaknesses, the mistakes and sins of omission which occurred then as they do in every age and which we will never be able to justify. On the whole, the missionaries were so absorbed in their work for Africa that they had neither the time nor the detachment to reflect on their work in a self-critical way. Certainly, there ought to have been more thinkers, critics and prophets.

"Secondly, I want to look at the historical setting. We have to see and to speak the whole historical truth. This applies also to our accusers; they must give themselves up to the whole truth. If they do so, now and then an accusation will come back to them like a boomerang. Let's take as an example of what I mean the speech Colonel Gaddafi, President of Libya, made to the Pan-African Conference at Benghazi on March 23, 1974. In this speech he called upon Africans to get rid of Christianity on the grounds that it had been used in Black Africa as a means of destroying the African man. To this Archbishop Bernard Yago of Abidjan replied correctly that the Muslims were hardly in a position to preach to the christian Churches about religious freedom and tolerance. History presents us with facts, he said, which should not be overlooked even in the discussions, desirable as these are, between Islam and Christianity. If Christians are to be reproached with having destroyed the African character, what was it the Muslims were doing in the 11th century when, under the pretext of a crusade, they broke up the Ghanaian Empire at the peak of its civilisation? Or in the 19th century when they conquered the southern Sudan, decimated the population and destroyed the native culture? Or even in the last decades of the 19th century, long after the white men had stopped trafficking in slaves, when they, the Muslims, were still taking away something like 80,000 slaves a year? The conclusion to be drawn from all this is that there has probably never been a religious community which has not been tied up with power in the course of history. All of us must be converted *now* and must finally recognise that we are children of the one God and Father of all.

"Marxism will serve as another example. It has established its rule in a whole string of African states, but it accuses the missions of having misused the schools in order to turn the pupils into Christians. This is what President Samora Machel said in his speech to 6,000 students and teachers, a speech quoted in *Tempo* of March 26, 1977. If this accusation is meant seriously, then why is Marxism an *obligatory* subject in all the schools in the Marxist states? And why are practising

Christians disadvantaged when it comes to filling public posts? An accusation made by people who are guilty of the same failing should not be taken too seriously!

"Now let's examine in some detail the historical truth of the charges which have been made. Of course it is true that the missionaries of old did not acknowledge African culture as much as they should have done, nor did they build their message upon it. This was because the Europeans at that time saw their own culture and their own religion in so bright a light that anything else seemed like night in comparison. However, one must not generalise here. The founders of the two greatest missionary institutes in Africa, Fr Libermann and Cardinal Lavigerie, gave their missionaries very modern-sounding instructions. Libermann, for instance, said: 'Do not judge at first sight and do not judge by what you have seen in Europe. Free yourselves from Europe, from its customs, from its spirit! Become Negroes with the Negroes. Do not form them in a European way, but leave to them what is their own. Let your attitude towards them be that of slaves to their masters . . .' In similar vein, Lavigerie wrote: 'You should let the elders tell all the old legends, the whole history of the tribe, the origin of mankind and of the world, the original revelation and, in general, everything which the christian doctrine of the unity of the human race could confirm . . .' Both founders gave strict orders to their missionaries to keep diaries and to write reports and in fact the results of this, the *Chronique trimestrielle* of the White Fathers and the *Bulletins mensuels* of the Holy Ghost Fathers occupy much bookshelf space. The missionaries of old were not unintelligent fools without any foresight who wanted to destroy ruthlessly all the cultural values and customs of the Africans. On the contrary, many of them had an extraordinarily good appreciation of the realities of life and serious attempts were made to bring about a mutual penetration and cross-fertilisation between Christianity and the African heritage. In spite of this, however, when it came to concrete questions of adaptation, the majority of missionaries had a negative attitude. Why was this? It was perhaps precisely because they were too much aware of the realities of life. The Africa of that time was perhaps not quite as idyllic as the ethnologists and Africans of today describe it. One has only to think of the slavery among the African tribes, of the poisonings, of the misuse of power by sorcerers, of the abuses of polygamy and child-marriage and of the cruelties practised against people of other tribes. The missionaries became simply disillusioned and alarmed. They compared all this with the relationships in the families in which they had grown up and they began to condemn what they saw in Africa. Is it not a general human weakness to regard one's own people as the best? Wasn't there, and isn't there still, even in Africa, a tribal selfishness which judges disapprovingly of other tribes?

"When it is said that the missions and colonialism went hand in hand, there again this statement would have to be qualified. It was only natural that the German, French and Belgian missionaries working in the colonies belonging to their respective countries should, normally, have a good relationship with the colonial officials who were their fellow-countrymen. However, it ought to be known that, although the missionaries in many cases opened up the country ahead of the colonialists, it was not for their benefit that they did so. Bagamoyo was already a flourishing mission-station by the time Stanley got together his caravan there for his trip into the African interior and the White Fathers had already been working for ten years in the land of the great lakes when Dr Peters roved through the area in order to conclude defensive alliances with the chieftains. Most missionaries looked forward to the coming of the white colonial power with mixed feelings. Soon there was any amount of friction and quarrelling in important and in less important matters alike. If the Africans considered they had been unjustly treated by the civil authorities, they were only too eager to complain to the missionaries and to ask them to intervene and to protect them. There was often harsh conflict because of different ideas on marriage and different ideas on educational policy. The not exactly exemplary private life of many white people and the harsh methods of many planters annoyed the missionaries just as the doctrine of the equality and the brotherhood of all men presented by the missionaries gave offence to many white people. What the officials found particularly unpleasant about all these conflicts was that the missionaries were not only constantly passing on these complaints to higher officials but that they were also bringing them to the attention of the public in their own countries by means of the missionary magazines. In this whole matter, then, one must avoid generalisations. Naturally, love for the Gospel and love for the Church were usually not so disinterested as to exclude a partiality towards one's own country, a partiality which sometimes reached the point of exaggerated nationalism.

"Now a word about the older views of faith and the older catechetical methods. In the wake of the Counter Reformation the Catholic Church had in fact over-emphasised certain points. The seven sacraments were regarded as the absolute centre of everything and the Bible was pushed into the background. Faith became a system of truths which had to be learned by heart from the Penny Catechism and trotted out in examinations. The almost magical notion of the sacraments as the sole effective means of salvation led many missionaries to a kind of obsession regarding Baptism of necessity. Many missionary magazines of that time are full of 'edifying' and partly downright grotesque stories in which missionary sisters in particular tell of how they managed 'to snatch from the devil's jaws' children and adults on the point of death and, by privately baptising them, to open to them the bliss of heaven. This basically terrifying conviction gave the missionaries an extraordinary power in the way they thought and acted. This sort of thing can in no way be justified by our present-day understanding of faith; at that time, however, this was how people in Europe thought and, hence, how people in Africa thought.

"I would like to say to Mr Horst Müller that his ideas about missionary propaganda in the past are partly correct; but things changed a long time ago. Such organisations as *Missio, Misereor, Adveniat* and *Fastenopfer* all provide a first-class information service. There is now extensive cooperation between the missionary institutes. Alas, one still finds the old ideas in force here and there rather like a fly-wheel which takes time to stop, but one has grounds for expecting that the young men of today won't peddle the old clichés.

"The attitude of rivalry which prevailed between the different christian Churches in Africa is and remains a depressing part of the story. Some regarded it as heroic to take school places from each other, to entice teachers and catechists away from one's rivals and even to set fire to their schools! It happened again and again that rivals slandered one another, charged each other with heresy and made accusations about them to the authorities. We can never boast about this. Even within the Catholic Church there was a pronounced coolness and distance between the missionary institutes. When Rome redistributed areas of work there was not infrequently tension and friction between the missionaries concerned. The arrival of new missionary societies was often felt to be a disagreeable interference in one's own sphere of work rather than a help. Among the different Protestant groups the disharmony was even more confusing because they had no set territorial boundaries and thus crossed one another even more.

"Mr President, such is the confession of guilt of the poor missionaries. What they are criticised for, they admit in a spirit of self-criticism, although with some corrections. But to do them justice, their virtues as well as their vices must be placed on the scales and then it will be shown which side tips the balance. Only both elements together constitute this peculiar phenomenon we call human, christian life.

"In making this last remark I am hinting at the theological setting into which, in the end, everything must be placed in order to gain, at least for believers, its ultimate meaning. In the course of history, from the Inquisition and the Crusades down to the defective methods and attitudes of the missionaries in Africa, many crude mistakes have been made in the name of a not very enlightened faith. On the other hand, in the name of true faith, innumerable acts of self-conquest and of sacrifice for one's neighbour amounting sometimes to heroism have been made. Both these aspects are taken up into the theology of the Incarnation, the Cross and the Resurrection. The Church has always experienced in herself human nature in all its ambivalence, human nature in its misery so that we suffer under the 'human' aspect of the Church; but we also see human nature in its beauty and greatness and so we are glad to live in a 'human' Church. Yet even failure and guilt, the dark stage of the Cross, are overcome and perfected in the power of God. Anyone who cannot see things in this way will not get to the root of the life of the missionaries and of the meaning of history.

"I will conclude with a challenge: 'Let him who is without sin cast the first stone'. Anyone who is 50 years ahead of his time may condemn those people of the past who were not able to do likewise. The rest of us keep silence and bow before the mystery of man in his greatness and in his limitations".

* * *

The President: "We are now going to hear Fritz Raaflaub, Ph.D. Dr Raaflaub is Swiss and a member of the Protestant Mission of Basle; he is a missionary and a scholar in missionary matters. From 1951 to 1976 he was an official adviser to the Basle Mission in Africa, from 1964 to 1976 President of the Swiss Evangelical Missionary

Council and in 1976 he was awarded an honorary doctorate of theology by the University of Basle. He is, as you see, a highly qualified man".

Fritz Raaflaub[14]: "Mr President, naturally we who are to speak in defence of the missions have talked among ourselves and worked out an order of points to be raised. It falls to me to make some remarks about the mission schools.

"In his standard work, *An African Survey*, which appeared in 1938, Lord Hailey wrote: 'It is impossible to present correctly the development of the educational system in Africa without acknowledging the pioneering achievements of the missions which introduced and developed in Africa schools and other forms of instruction'. In 1945 the same author proved that, even in that year, no less than 96.4 per cent of all schoolchildren in each of the British territories in Africa were in mission-schools. How did the missions come to be so involved in the educational system? What did they achieve by this involvement? These are the questions I now want to investigate.

"In the work of the missions in Africa, school and church went hand in hand like twin sisters as if things had to be that way. The missionaries almost everywhere began to instruct the young without lengthy reflection as to whether they ought to do so. In the vast majority of cases the first school sprang up soon after the arrival of the missionaries and it often happened that the number of schools increased much more quickly than did the number of parishes and that the number of pupils was much greater than that of the baptised Church members. The great pioneer of the missions in the Cameroons, Alfred Saker, who went to Duala 40 years before the beginning of the German colonial period, founded many schools. When the first mission-station in Barotseland was established in 1882, a schoolhouse was built at the

[14] The text was written by F. Raaflaub.

same time as a house for the missionary. For most missions, Evangelical and Catholic alike, the setting-up of a so-called out-station meant also the establishment of an elementary school. The few missions which tried to function without schools were forced to recognise before long that in Africa you couldn't get anywhere without them. This powerful movement of opening schools was based on the following facts:

(a) The missions saw the Gospel as a force leading not only to a new attitude but also to a change in one's way of living. The proclamation of the Gospel had to be accompanied by down-to-earth witness — by medical help, by training in agriculture and crafts. Now the basis for this was the school.

(b) For the missions — especially for the Evangelical missions — it was taken for granted that Christians should have direct access to the Bible. This presumed the ability to read.

(c) It was equally obvious that, as soon as possible, natives should be trained as preachers; so at first so-called helpers — usually known by the name 'catechist' or 'catechete' — were trained and, later, parsons and priests. Now this presumed not only theological colleges or indeed, at a later date, theological faculties, but first of all schools for everybody.

(d) For other reasons too the missions were interested in young people: God's gift of Jesus Christ in the Gospel was made to them just as much as to the adults. The missionaries were convinced that the most suitable vehicle for presenting this offer to them was the school. The school became even more important when it proved difficult, in some places, to win over the adults. In fact, time and again the school became the wellspring of the community when older pupils received Baptism. The missionaries tried to reach the parents through the pupils and gradually to influence public life.

(e) Finally, one may not hush up the fact that in Europe in the last century people were convinced that christian culture had a universal validity and that it should be handed on to the peoples of Africa through the schools. Since that time everyone has been completely cured of this cultural optimism, but at the beginning of the classical age of the missions, indeed even up to the First World War, this attitude was decisive.

"Thus mission-schools were set up; their basis was usually a dense network of elementary village schools with two or three classes. A mud hut served as schoolhouse and church and the village teacher was preacher and catechist rolled into one. His general education was meagre. The curriculum consisted of Bible history, reading, writing, arithmetic, singing and, if the teacher's knowledge stretched that far, a little natural science.

"Soon more advanced schools became necessary. Proper primary schools were opened, at first in the mission-stations and then, little by little, in other bigger centres of population. In these schools, the language of the colonial power was not just a subject in the curriculum, it was the language in which the teaching was done. For a long time these schools were boarding-schools because great importance was attached to christian presence in everyday communal living. These schools produced clerks who worked for the authorities, for trading firms and for planters as well as teachers in the missions or students for entry into a training college. Quite early on many missionaries founded colleges for the training of teachers and preachers together. The teacher training college at Akropong in Ghana, later to become famous, was opened in 1848, only five years after the second beginning of the work of the Basle Mission. In the Cameroons a similar college was opened twelve years after the arrival of the first missionaries.

"Before the Second World War there were only very few higher middle schools which qualified people for university entrance or for senior positions in the civil service. In the midst of this struggle of the nations, in which thousands of Africans took part, people began to speak not only of the 'battle for the freedom of the world' but also of the coming independence of the colonies in Asia and Africa, and the African peoples were seized by a real hunger for education.

"The number of primary schools grew enormously, principally through the work of the missions, although more and more of the cost was paid for by the state. The elementary village schools gradually folded up or were developed to become primary schools. In addition there sprang up in quick succession very many secondary schools and grammar schools and a network of teacher training colleges. In the former British Cameroons, for instance, before 1940 there was only one Catholic secondary school; eventually there were 12, of which only one was owned by the state. This development was repeated in almost all the British territories and, to a lesser extent, in the areas of French influence. The founding of universities, which also began after the Second World War, was taken in hand by the governments.

"At first, the European colonial authorities showed little concern either about the education of youth or about what the missions were doing for them. In 1910, in the German colonies, a set of regulations was drawn up giving guidelines for the curriculum and for the financial assistance to be given to schools in which German was taught. In England, an advisory committee for educational questions in Africa was set up in 1926. Very soon this committee issued a statement of basic principles and tried even later on to further the educational system in British terrorities by important publications.

"Thus, as time went on, a degree of partnership between the missions and the colonial authorities was achieved. In British colonies, in accordance with English tradition, great importance was attached to religious education. The Church-schools were highly regarded and soon began to receive financial assistance provided they kept to certain guidelines regarding the curriculum and met minimum requirements for buildings and apparatus. The tuition fees plus the official subsidies were usually sufficient to maintain the schools and pay the teachers' salaries. New buildings had to be paid for by the missions which could, even here, count on an appreciable subsidy from the state.

"Conditions in the French territories were less favourable. Here, as in France itself, the lay system existed, that is, a system according to which, in principle, there is no religious instruction in the schools. Hence it was that the mission-schools were tolerated rather than welcomed and they received a correspondingly lower amount in subsidies. However, in the whole of Africa south of the Sahara, the educational system of the missionaries was predominant to the end of the colonial period and even beyond it.

"Thus it came about that the majority of educated Africans in the colonial period owed their education to the missions. Almost all the political leaders who led their countries to independence and became ministers in the new states had gone through the mission-schools, and this was often publicly admitted. Kwame Nkrumah, the first President of Ghana, was speaking for many when he said, not long after the independence celebrations: 'It is the missionaries who have really brought Africa to life. I and many others are everything we are because of their work and their help'. At many independence celebrations the importance of the mission-schools in the achieving of independence by the colonies was explicitly pointed out. In fact, the very unpretentious village schools started a process which could never be arrested — the awakening of Africa.

"It is sad, but it is a fact, that the schools often became a bone of contention between the christian denominations because it was through the schools that the goodwill of a chief and access to a village were won. But this unfortunate rivalry has, on the whole, given way to a spirit of cooperation, especially since the Second Vatican Council.

"The curricula presented a particularly difficult problem. For a long time, the only attention paid to African culture was that in the village schools the teaching was done in the language of the country and that the content of the reading books in the early years was taken from the world in which the children lived and from the legends of the country. Apart from this, the European curricula were adopted; in the higher schools this was entirely the case. In the French-speaking colonies things went so far that in the higher schools the same history books were used as in France. For many years the conditions for final examinations were exactly the same as those in London or Paris. This was not the fault of the missions, it was due to the international complications of the higher educational system with regard to preparation for university entrance.

"The criticism is rightly made nowadays that the Africans were alienated in this way from their own culture, but present-day critics would hardly have acted differently in that situation, indeed they would hardly have been able to. It is also true that it took a long time for the Africans in the inescapable conflict of cultures to become aware of their own identity and to discover the values of their own culture. We must not, however, overlook the fact that traditional African culture had, as well as very many positive aspects, its negative sides and these could not simply be carried over into the new age.

"Many attempts were made to bring the school curricula more in line with conditions in Africa, but it was not until the education conference of the independent African states in Addis Ababa in 1961 that the problems of education in Africa in the future were thoroughly discussed. This conference demanded that drastic steps be taken, that much greater attention be paid to native culture; it stressed equally the importance of scientific and technical education. It is difficult to find the correct balance in this matter and even now one essential concern of this conference has only begun to be taken into consideration, viz., the cultivation of the native language. It was a tragedy that after the Second World War, because of the rush to develop the educational system and because, later, the newly-formed states were trying hard to fuse the many tribes into one nation, the local languages were replaced by European languages even in the earliest stages of schooling. Alienation through the schools was thus intensified and only slowly did the africanisation of the educational system get under way.

"What happened next? Since the decolonisation of Africa much has changed. In many countries the whole educational system has been taken over by the state; elsewhere, in Ghana and the Cameroons for example, the Churches are still heavily involved. But how long will this go on? In 1963 it was said: 'Education is in no way a secondary concern of the christian Churches; it is at the heart of the christian Gospel which urges Christians to seek the truth in obedience to Christ and to see to it that young people are brought up according to his will in family, school and other institutions'. Nowadays many Church leaders would agree with the second but not necessarily with the first part of this statement. The schools are beginning to become a burden. By no means every church school is a place where christian witness is given. This depends entirely on the teachers of whom many are nominal rather than deeply convinced Church members. Administrative work demands a lot of time and energy and in some places there are financial problems. One gets the impression that the Churches and the missions have completed their task as pioneers of the educational system in Africa and could now well hand over full responsibility for it to the state. The question remains whether or not the Churches should keep just a few private schools with staffs of really convinced christian teachers to set a standard as it were. The Churches would also have to be concerned with the provision of well trained teachers of religious instruction in the state schools where this is possible. This is still the normal practice in countries influenced by British traditions, even in Northern Nigeria which has a strong Muslim influence.

"This much, however, is beyond dispute: Africa would not be where it is at the present time were it not for the educational work of the christian missions".

* * *

The President: "Our next speaker is Sr Joan Delaney of the Maryknoll Missionaries, an American congregation. Sr Delaney is Secretary General of *Sedos*, which is a working-party made up of representatives from 50 Catholic missionary institutes and based in Rome. Prior to this appointment she taught in Hong Kong".

Sr Joan Delaney[15]: "Mr President, the great concern and the great hope of the African nations is liberation — from ignorance, from sickness and from poverty. These three enemies go hand in hand and together drive people into a tight spot from which there is hardly any hope of escape. Because they are ignorant, people do not know the basic rules of hygiene, they know nothing about healthier feeding-habits and fall an easy prey to sickness. Because they are sick, they have not enough energy for regular work and so they remain poor. Because they are poor, individuals have no money with which to lead a better life and the country has no money with

[15] The account, which has been examined by Sr Delaney, is based mainly on: *A propos de l'action médicale en Afrique*, PMV, Centrum Informationis, no. 21 (Brussels 1967) and *The healing ministry*, International Review of Mission, no. 226 (Geneva 1968).

which to develop the educational system. So people remain in ignorance and the sad story begins all over again.

"For more than a century the christian missions have done their utmost to break through this vicious circle of misery and to give the people new hope. We have just heard what has been achieved in the field of education; we must now show how the missions have attacked the second enemy, sickness.

"For decades almost all missionaries doubled as nurses and doctors. At that time the colonial authorities were not equipped to organise a comprehensive health service, but the missionaries, who were here, there and everywhere, saw the sufferings of the people and had to do something. Their medical knowledge was relatively meagre but their dedication wasn't, so they set about the task and healed innumerable sick people with their ointments and medicines. On their part it was a quite natural reaction of christian love for one's neighbour. They were doing simply what Christ did; he not only showed compassion for the sick, he also healed them. It is striking that Christ always gave his disciples a threefold commission: to drive out devils, that is, to free men from all psychological pressure; to cure sickness, which means to overcome all bodily misery; and to proclaim the Good News, that is, to give man something definite to hope for in this life and even in death. The healing ministry is then to be regarded as an essential part of the work of Christ and of his Church. The independent Churches in Africa take this more seriously than anyone else; the community prays for those members who are sick and cures really do take place whatever the explanation for them may be — suggestion? magnetism? miracle?

"The missions carried out their healing ministry in different stages. It began with 'first-aid' when primitive means were used as effectively as possible in the circumstances. The next stage was that of 'works', the well-developed schools and hospitals. For decades the missions were the primary and almost the only source from which nurses and doctors came. The missions opened and conducted the first nursing schools. In these schools they were the first to use scientific knowledge to combat superstition and magic, to combat a way of thought which was the cause of the defeatist attitude of the people. Present-day developments in the health service would have been impossible without this laborious, thorough and hidden work done by the missionaries.

"One ought to sing the praises of hundreds of nurses and doctors. Dr Schweitzer and Dr Goarnission are only two prominent tips of an iceberg. All the others — and there are very many of them — are not exposed to publicity; the thanks they receive is the shining eyes of those they have healed. To make a man whole is a wonderful, a divine work!

"It is very difficult to measure this quiet working in terms of statistics since statistics are never complete and reliable. Under the pressure of life in Africa there is little room available for bureaucracy. Nonetheless, it can be said that the Churches are among the greatest supporters of hospitals in the world. It is estimated that the Protestant and Anglican Churches own 1,228 hospitals and 300 nursing schools in 85 countries of the Third World and a considerable number of these are in Africa. Not many years ago, the Catholic Church was running, in Africa, 625 hospitals with 81,403 beds and 763 maternity hospitals as compared with 534 state-owned hospitals. Catholic sisters, as well as working in their own hospitals, were also working in many owned by the state. In the Congo, for instance, in 1959, out of 145 state-owned hospitals 117 were run by Catholic sisters.

"Now in stating all this, we do not wish to boast, for the left hand should not know what the right hand is doing. We are, however, involved in a lawsuit in which a judgement has to be made about the existence or non-existence of the missions and so we have a duty to demonstrate that the failings with which the missions are being charged never outweigh the great deal of good they have done.

"For many years now the governments have taken over the principal responsibility for the health services. The missions do not object to this. On the contrary, they are ready to join the health services provided by the state authorities, who depend on good and reliable personnel. The task is still a vast one. The child mortality rate in Africa is still, on average, 10.3 per cent. Even now there are 10 million lepers, 15 million TB patients, 100 million cases of malaria each year and the same number of infectious intestinal diseases caused by worms and amoebae.

"A writer on missionary affairs confessed to me that he is almost embarrassed when he travels through Africa and sees how the bulk of the people have only one meal a day, how at night they are unprotected against mosquitoes, how they bear their misery and their sicknesses with patience. In Africa, he said, even to live is an heroic act, but people there live without heroism, in a matter-of-fact way, even joyfully. These people have to be admired, he concluded, but they also have to be helped.

"The authorities can count on us then. We don't want to defend our hospitals, all we want to do is to help the people. Perhaps too we can help prevent corruption, because far too many nursing staff demand bribes for injections and medicines which should be handed out at no cost to the patient. In addition, we would like to offer sick people a comprehensive treatment, that is to say, not to restrict ourselves to giving them a scientific examination and technical help but to be close to them as human beings and to inspire them with hope and confidence.

"Mr President, this is what I mean when I say that the Churches or the missions still have a complementary role to play in the state health system and that together we can carry out our work as Samaritans to help all those who lie by the roadside beaten, wounded and helpless".

* * *

Tuesday, June 3

First Vice-President: "Once again we have a woman to address us. This time it is an 80-year-old woman, Sr Marie-André du Sacré-Coeur, a White Sister. Perhaps not everyone is aware of what she has done for women's rights and for the advancement of women in Africa. Let us listen to her with the respect Africans always show towards women and elderly people".

Amid applause and visibly moved, quickly and yet a little uncertainly, Sr Marie-André makes her way to the speaker's desk. Dressed all in white, with thin fingers, a pale — almost transparent — face and sparkling eyes, she stands there like someone who has come back from the other world to deliver a message.

Sr Marie-André [16]: "Mr President, over the past fifty years I have made many speeches and this will probably be my last one. In all my lectures, articles and books I have always spoken about and on behalf of African women with a view to helping them win their rights. My present task is to speak about us sisters and other missionaries with a view to helping us win our disputed rights. As a Doctor of Laws I cannot sit back and do nothing when I see anyone's rights under fire. Everything in me urges me on to help the right get what is due to it.

"Nowadays African women play a quite consider-

[16] The text has been compiled from various books of Sr Marie-André, from her article, *Promotion féminine et familiale* in the Revue du Clergé Africain, from conversations with her, with Sr Marie Lorin of the Generalate of the White Sisters and with Sr Anne-Marie Kerneis, a member of the Secretariate of the International Union of Women Religious Superiors General with special responsibility for Africa.

able role in modern society; there are trained female nurses, teachers, social workers; the women of Africa are represented on local authorities, in Parliament, in international organisations and at international conferences. In order to appreciate this remarkable development properly we must turn back the pages of history several decades.

"In 1932 I received an urgent request from missionaries of both sexes in French West Africa to go there and make a study of the position of women, because the missionaries had almost given up hope of ever producing christian families from African society. If I might be permitted to sum up all our efforts since that time I would say: the African girl, the African wife and the African widow have been liberated.

"Traditional African society was concerned primarily that women should survive, that they should produce children and that they should have a social value; it was not so much concerned about their dignity as persons. A young woman did not belong to herself, nor even to her father but, according to circumstances, to certain elders of the clan, who entered into business deals over her and got paid for so doing! They made business deals over minors as well and even over unborn children whom they gave in marriage to prominent men even though these sometimes already had more than one wife. Widows were treated similarly. I have made a study of these relationships and have compared them with ancient Roman and with Germanic law and I have discovered very many points of similarity. Because of this, these customs cannot simply be regarded as bad, although it is true that they were not in accord with modern developments, with women's increasing self-awareness and with their full rights as persons. These old customs had to be stripped off just as the grass-skirt had to be replaced by modern dress.

"I have put forward my reflections in articles, books and at meetings with the aim of influencing public opinion in Africa and in the major cities of the West. But ideas take time to sink through; walls will simply not be bulldozed; growth has to come from within. In 1939 I, a woman, was able to present my case to a commission of the French Chamber of Deputies and to ask for a corresponding law to be passed. The very same year my idea took on flesh in the Mandel Decree, which was applied immediately in the whole of French West and Central Africa. The principal item in this decree was that henceforward a girl or a widow should have the right to accept or reject the deals made by the elders, in other words, that henceforward marriage should depend on the express consent of the parties concerned. This was the first and decisive step towards the emancipation of women. The missions now aimed, in educating girls, to give them the courage to say a decisive 'No' before a judge in certain circumstances; these girls were still so intimidated that they hardly dared contradict the opinion of the elders. But gradually the new freedom became the normal thing.

"The first encroachment upon tradition had the effect of a spreading oil-stain. Little by little girls and women began to get organised. They themselves began to demand full equality and marriage legislation which respected their dignity and, among other things, abolished the misuse of dowries. Polygamy also cannot count on continuing in the future. Some countries have officially abolished it, others have resolved on temporary solutions. In 1975, on the occasion of International Women's Year, a Congress of African Women was held in Lomé. I was surprised and delighted to receive from the organising committee an official invitation to this congress. What a difference between the mental attitude of women then and now! Marriage cannot be put in order simply by legislation, it has to develop; above all, the awareness both of wife and of husband has to develop and we know from the history of civilisation that a civilisation stands and falls with the family.

"Even now there is still a lot to be put right and

new problems are cropping up. The movement of African women cannot be said without more ado to have the same objectives as the women's movements in the West where the struggle is going on for the right to abortion, to free love, to homosexual love. African women have not yet been completely freed from subjection to self-centred men, from living in slums, from working a 15 hour day, from unjust wages, from superstition. But they will succeed and will, before long, have the same rights as men 'before marriage, during marriage and after marriage' as Article 16 of the Declaration of Human Rights demands. Women still have undiscovered treasures of love, of dedication, of intuition, of humanity, of christ-likeness which need to be developed. State and Church in Africa must really care about wives and mothers; if they do this, they will have put their future into good hands".

The speaker stops; she takes a deep breath, but gives no indication she is going to leave the platform. After a while, she glances at the President and begins again.

"Mr President, I have still one more aspect of the question of women to deal with. I would ask you to grant me another quarter of an hour to present what is perhaps the most beautiful chapter in the recent history of Africa. I am referring to the story of the black sisters. Their beginnings remind one of the wonderful vision described in the 35th chapter of Isaiah, when the prophet sees the dead and desperate desert suddenly begin to turn green; it bursts into flower and a stream bubbles forth. In a similar way black girls, who until that time had shared the lot of all women in Africa, have suddenly discovered a new way, have received new hope. At one time they would bashfully say to the white sisters, 'we would like to be like you'. These were girls who had already been promised in marriage to prominent men, who had to fight against their parents who stood to lose the bride-price, and all this because they wished to lead celibate lives in order to be able to serve God and their fellow-men without reserve.

"At the Congress of Congregations of African Sisters held in Lomé in 1970 an African priest complained bitterly that there had been no really great religious founders in Africa, that the white sisters had founded congregations in order to have black servants, that European dress, the nun's veil and monastic customs had been transplanted to Africa without prior reflection, and so on. It is certainly not our intention to disprove all the accusations made, but one thing is supported by facts, viz., the initiative in all this came not from the white sisters but from the black girls and, ultimately, from the Holy Spirit. The first instance of this is quite typical. In 1886 Maria-Mathilde Munaka, sister of one of the Uganda martyrs, came along to a mission-station and said: 'My brother has been killed because he prayed. I too would like to pray'. She asked to be allowed to remain at the mission-station. After some time she was baptised and consecrated herself to God by a private vow. At first she looked after orphans and in 1903 took charge of the cooking and housekeeping in the minor seminary at Kisubi. She died in 1934.

"My own congregation, the White Sisters, admitted the first black girls to profession in 1907. Over the years, in the different areas where our sisters work, 17 independent congregations of sisters have grown up. At first we were in charge of them but, as time went on, the black sisters took on more and more responsibility. In 1975 these 17 congregations had a total of 3,195 members. We do not patronise them; all we do is to lend a hand here and there — for example, with in-service-training courses — or we work with them in other ways just as we do with congregations of white sisters. In 1976 there were in 28 African countries, as far as we can tell, 116 generalates of African sisters. These sisters — and we don't know how many of them there are — work in schools, hospitals, homes, parishes, and are involved in girls and women's movements. When one thinks of the Africa of today, one cannot think of it without them; they are glowing examples of liberated women and some of them have led a truly saintly life of prayer and self-sacrifice.

"In 1954 there was set up in Rome the 'Regina Mundi', an international institute of theology affiliated to the Gregorian University; here sisters from Asia and Africa can take a diploma in theology and spirituality. In recent years there has been an average of 30 to 40 African sisters studying at 'Regina Mundi'. The raising of the professional and theological standard is having a noticeably positive effect in that these sisters, who previously felt inferior, have become more self-confident, more open in discussion and have acquired a much deeper richness in their inner life. The progress made is seen clearly in the general assemblies of the International Union of Superiors General of Women's Institutes which are held in Rome every three years. The last general assembly — in 1976 — was attended by 18 African sisters. They had no more feelings of inferiority but regarded themselves and were regarded by the others as equals who enriched each other. There was general recognition of the charming and valuable contribution made by the African sisters.

"Mr President, I thank you for your patience and I thank God that I have lived to see this development. The sun has risen over Africa. The African woman, the African sister, have something to give not only to Africa but to the whole world and to the whole Church. The riches of creation and of God's grace are being revealed more and more. I look forward to the future with joy".

During this speech not only the audience was keyed-up, even the council of elders dropped its customary reserve and applauded enthusiastically. This was not the despondent vision of a weary person, it was not a eulogy of the good old days, it was the witness of a woman who was in the thick of things, who was playing an active part in events, who was preparing the future with faith in the future. Sr Marie-André, somewhat tired, a little excited, yet smiling, now leaves the speaker's desk. In no time she is surrounded by cheering black women and sisters. It is the most wonderful day of her life.

* * *

First Vice-President: "By way of contrast to the lively and warmhearted lady we have just heard, we now listen to a speaker with a more academic topic. Professor Hugo Huber, a Swiss member of the Divine Word Missionaries, lectures at the University of Fribourg in Switzerland and is a member of the Anthropos Institute which has published the *Internationale Fachzeitschrift für Linguistik und Ethnologie* since 1906. Dr Huber is going to tell you about the contribution made by the missions to the scientific investigation of Africa".

Professor Hugo Huber[17]*:* "Mr President, the topic I have been given is so vast that I can hardly see the forest for the trees. What I really ought to do is to take you all into a library of books dealing exclusively with Africa and then conduct a practical experiment with you. What I would do would be to remove from that library all the books on linguistics, ethnology and culture written by Catholic or Protestant missionaries; you would then see with your own eyes that the contents of the library had been halved! Above all the earliest contributions on which later research was able to build are mainly the work of the missionaries. It is quite impossible in a short space of time to give even a relatively complete account of what these missionaries have achieved in the way of the scientific study of Africa. They have not just made one trip and done a few months field-work, they have spent a lifetime among the people, they have become a

[17] Professor Huber provided the material for this speech.

part of the people and have made a careful record of everything they came across in the way of linguistic and cultural riches and have thus made them available to science and to posterity. All I can do is to give you an incomplete and dull list of some names which have been particularly outstanding. I shall restrict myself to linguistics and ethnology and will leave out of consideration the equally valuable contributions made in the fields of geography and cartography, botany and zoology.

"Even the early missions in the Congo provide us with a classical case. From 1645 to 1865 Capuchin missionaries worked in the old Congo kingdom which extended — in present-day terms — from Brazzaville past Kinshasa to the north of Angola. To these missionaries we owe a mine of information about the language, customs, usages and history of the Bakongo tribe. Professor T. Filesi has set out this rich material in his recent book. It emerges from this book that in the early period the Capuchins wrote and printed six books on history and culture and four on language (a grammar, a dictionary and a catechism). In more recent times critical editions have been made of nine large and twelve smaller works which had never before been printed. In addition, different archives in Italy contain a vast number of letters which Filesi has listed and catalogued. The Bakongo know of their past only from the accounts written by the Capuchins.

"In the last century, a new period of missionary activity began in Africa and, once again, the missionaries were among the earliest philologists. The Evangelical missionaries came before the Catholics. Koelle in Sierra Leone, for instance, compiled his *Polyglotta Africana,* a comparative list of short vocabularies of West African languages, in 1854; Bennie John in 1826 published a vocabulary and as a result is known as 'the father of Kaffir literature'. We may mention also — J.G. Christaller, whose life will be recalled in a speech tomorrow; D. Westermann, who published a dictionary and a grammar of the Ewe language of Togo and then, on the basis of his many studies of the Sudanese languages and of general African philology, became one of the great experts; J. Ittmann, who made a study of the Nyang language in the Cameroons; and J. Zimmermann, who wrote a grammar and a dictionary of the Ga language of Ghana. There were many others too.

"Among the Catholic missionaries, the Holy Ghost Father, Charles Sacleux, was particularly outstanding. He went to East Africa in 1879 and became a great expert on Swahili. Not only did he publish a great number of religious books in this language but he also wrote a grammar in which all the differences in the dialects were noted, a French-Swahili dictionary (1891) and a two-volume Swahili-French dictionary which appeared in 1939 as the fruit of more than 40 years work. Other names worthy of mention include those of the White Father, A. Probst, publisher of studies of the Mande, Sonay and Volta languages of West Africa; the Lyons missionary, J. Bertho, who wrote on the Volta languages and that of Dogon; the Sacred Heart Missionaries G. Hulstaert, A. de Rop and E. Boelaert on the Nkundo-Mongo language of Zaire; the Scheutfeld Missionary P. de Witte on the language of the Basakata tribe of Zaire and the Capuchin G. Maes on the Ngbaka language also of Zaire.

"But language is only a means of understanding men and their culture. Many Protestant churchmen and missionaries have published excellent studies on African culture and religion. Among these are H.A. Junod, on the Thonga of Mozambique; B. Gutmann, on the Dschaga of Tanzania; J. Spieth, on the Ewe of Togo; W. Ringwald, on the Akan of Ghana; A. Hauenstein, on the Ovimbundu and the Hanya of Angola; H. Debrunner, on the remaining peoples of Togo and G. Parrinder, E.W. Smith and B. Sundkler, who published various studies on African religions.

"Among the Catholic missionaries one might mention

the Jesuits J. van Wing and Y. Struyf, with their studies on the Bakongo; E. Lamal, L. de Beir and M. Plancquaert, on the Bayaka and the Basuku of Zaire; E. de Decker, on the Bambundu of Zaire; de Sousberghe, on the Bapende of Zaire; H.M. Dubois, on the Betsileo of Madagascar; the White Fathers M. Pauwels and D. Nothomb, on the culture and religion of Rwanda and A. Shorter, on the Kimbu.

"The Verona Father J.P. Crazzolara wrote on the Luo of the Sudan, and the Divine Word Missionaries P. Schumacher, P. Schebesta and M. Gusinde did research on the pygmies. For some years Fr Hermann Hochegger has been working with a team of Zairese at the *Centre d'études ethnologiques de Bandundu* in Zaire on the systematic recording of traditional stories. So far, more than 3,000 stories have been recorded in the local languages and filed away in 38 manuscript volumes. Of these 22 volumes have been published.

"Mr President, let me repeat; the list of names and works I have given is far from complete. It can be supplemented, perhaps, by the conclusions of specialists. The German ethno-sociologist, Richard Thurnwald, did not hesitate to describe the old missionary magazines as a mine of ethnographical information (cf. *Africa* 1931, p. 418), and Sir F.D. Lugard, on the occasion of the founding of the International Africa Institute in London, expressed the hope that the Institute might draw much profit from the great knowledge of the Protestant and Catholic missionaries and their familiarity with the people in Africa. In judging the missionaries, such testimony should not be ignored".

* * *

First Vice-President: "Our next speaker is Doctor the Reverend Ulrich Fick, Secretary General of the Protestant United Bible Societies based in Stuttgart".

Ulrich Fick[18]: "Mr President, I am able to report to you on what is probably the most wonderful event in the contemporary Church, viz., the joint efforts being made by the Protestant Bible Societies and the Catholic Church in the translation and dissemination of the Bible.

"To estimate the importance of this statement, let us recall the 'good old days' when the popes up to and including Leo XIII condemned the Protestant Bible Societies which came into being at that time and numbered them among the greatest errors of the age; when Catholics took it for granted that our Bible translations were deliberately falsified, and hence were forbidden by the Code of Canon Law (can. 1399) to read Protestant Bibles. We, on the other hand, were convinced that the Catholic missionaries had done nothing towards translating the Bible into the languages of the missionary countries because they celebrated the liturgy only in Latin and taught the catechism; in other words, they proclaimed not God's word but man's.

"These opinions and this state of affairs have now faded away like a bad dream. In 1959 Fr Walter M. Abbott in the United States and Fr Walbert Bühlmann writing in the Swiss publication *Neue Zeitschrift für Missionswissenschaft* quite independently of one another launched the bold idea that the Churches should stop working against each other and should work with each other in order to give the world the book to which it was entitled. This announcement caused both surprise and joy in Protestant circles. We asked ourselves: Does this, like the arrival of the swallows, herald spring? Or is it an idea in the minds of Catholic eccentrics only? The Second Vatican Council removed all doubts. It became clear to us from the constitution *On Divine Revelation*

[18] The text is based on J. Beckmann, W. Bühlmann, J. Specker, editors of *Die Heilige Schrift in den katholischen Missionen* (Schöneck 1966), O. Béguin: *Roman Catholicism and the Bible* (London 1963) and E. Dammann: *Die Ubersetzung der Bibel in afrikanischen Sprachen.* It has been examined by U. Fick.

that Catholic and Protestant understanding of Scripture overlapped to a large extent. Following on from this, working together with separated brethren was not only allowed but almost recommended (n. 22). Meanwhile a series of articles in the *Neue Zeitschrift für Missionswissenschaft* (published separately in 1966) proved to us that the Catholic missions in no way worked without the Bible; on the contrary, they had, for example, already translated the New Testament into 26 African languages. The new spring was really and truly beginning.

"After various meetings of the pioneers, the time had come for official encounters which would hasten practical collaboration. On January 5, 1967, 10 representatives of the Bible Societies and 13 Catholic scholars met in Rome at the Secretariat for Christian Unity. On this occasion Cardinal Bea declared: 'It is no exaggeration to say that the possibility of our close cooperation ranks among the most important events in the present history of Christianity'. In 1968 there were published communally worked out guidelines for interconfessional collaboration in the translation of the Bible and finally we moved the headquarters both of the United Bible Societies from London and of the World Catholic Federation for the Biblical Apostolate from Rome to Stuttgart. The purpose of this was so that we could keep in closer and continual contact, that we could keep each other constantly supplied with information and that we could collaborate as effectively as possible in the work of translation, printing, dissemination and overall planning.

"This change at the centre very soon reached the outlying areas. It was as if it had been expected, it was simply in the air. Since then, united Bible Weeks have been held in many African countries, united Bible Services are always taking place, and here and there joint Bible Societies have been set up. In Africa at the present time there are 78 interconfessional translations or revisions of the Bible under way, a development which even optimists could never have foreseen.

"Our only desire is to present Africa with the Bible, to have it translated into all the African languages and to make the Gospel present in every part of Africa. The ability among young people and adults to read and write is increasing at such an astonishing — I would almost say alarming — rate that the printing and distribution of the Bible cannot keep pace with it. And yet we cannot sit back and watch Africans learning to read unless we offer them at the same time the book of books. For us it is an obligation of conscience to proclaim the Gospel message. We force it on no one, but on the other hand we have no right to withhold it from anyone. What happens when we have presented the Bible is one of God's mysteries and also up to man's free choice.

"Having said all this, we are at the beginning of a new era. The Bible is on the point of leading Christians back to their common foundations and to their original unity. It is on the point of becoming the book of the world. No matter what this world may look like in the future, the Bible will continue even in the third millennium to be the book most widely read by men whether it is read openly or in secret, for nothing else can satisfy man's longing for light, hope and salvation. In Africa the reading of the Bible is greeted with applause. Everywhere we come across a great hunger for the Word of God. No authority in the world has either the right or the power to suppress this book or to obstruct a collaboration which aims at crossing all boundaries and races and presenting it to the world.

"E. Dammann has rightly pointed out an interesting fact. In the territory which was Ancient Egypt and in Ethiopia too there were popular translations of the Bible, but there were none in the Maghrib, that is, the area stretching from Libya to Morocco. Was it purely accidental, he asks, that Christianity survived in the former but not in the latter countries? Whatever truth there may be in this, it must not happen in Africa that Christianity dies out through lack of Bibles. This is why we are making great efforts now to spread the book of books as widely as possible. If we succeed in our aim, then we can imitate the farmer in the Gospel and go home, eat and sleep. The seed that has been sown will germinate and spring up, it will bear fruit by itself and suddenly it will be harvest time".

* * *

Wednesday, June 4

Second Vice-President: "Our first speaker today is Paul R. Clifford, an Anglican from Selly Oak College in Birmingham and a committee member of the International Association for Mission Studies. It was at Selly Oak that Professor Groves taught for many years; Groves was the editor of a four-volume history of the growth of Christianity in Africa, a work which gives a fully ecumenical picture of Evangelical and Catholic missions".

Paul R. Clifford: "Mr President, the missions are here on trial and certain circles are hoping they will be liquidated. In one sense they will find that their hope has a foundation in the history of the missions for already the missions in Africa have twice begun and twice disappeared. The first period — in North Africa — lasted for six centuries. At that time, in that part of Africa, there was a well-organised Church with hundreds of bishops, but this Church was wiped out by Islam. The second period lasted three centuries and began when the missionaries came with the Portuguese sailors and worked in West Africa, the kingdom of Congo and in East Africa. But this mission too, hampered by the unfavourable climate and by lack of reinforcements dwindled to very small numbers in the middle of the last century. However, it had scarcely reached the low-water mark when there followed — as flow succeeds ebb — the third period with its more wide-ranging and more deep-seated effect, and we have good reason for assuming that the present Church in

Africa will never disappear. Our revered Professor Groves has described all this in great detail.

"We have heard a lot about the achievements of the missions in the fields of education, medicine, scholarly research and biblical translation. Now all this has not taken place in a vacuum; it is the work of men of flesh and blood, men endowed with courage and hope, figures whom we could display in a long portrait gallery, figures of men and women who have risked everything to proclaim the Gospel to Africa and who, in the process of doing so, have made a careful study of Africa and have built for Africa the foundations of a new era. We would like to acquaint you with at least some of these figures. We will deal with Protestants and Catholics separately rather than together for the technical reason that otherwise a single speaker would take up too much time. I will confine my attention to four personalities from the early pioneering days.[19]

"Let's begin with a man who explored a great part of southern Africa in the name of the Gospel. David Livingstone was born in Blantyre, Scotland, on March 19, 1813. While he was a young factory worker he learned Latin and attended night-school; then he studied medicine and theology. In 1841 he went to South Africa in the service of the London Missionary Society. At various places he trained Africans to preach the Gospel. His main interest, however — one could almost call it his indomitable passion — was the exploration of the at-that-time completely unknown African interior. Thus it was that he undertook ever greater journeys of exploration and became, in 1849, the first white man to reach Lake Nyami. In order to be more free for his work he sent his family back to England. Between 1851 and 1856 he made the first great journey of discovery along the River Zambesi to the gigantic falls which he named in honour of the English queen, the Victoria Falls, then to the source of the river and beyond

[19] The four short biographies were chosen and written by F. Raaflaub of the Basle Mission.

that to Luanda, the capital of Angola, and back again to East Africa. In England he was celebrated as a great explorer and showered with honours. His book *Missionary Travels and Researches in South Africa* became a best-seller. A speech he made in Cambridge provided the impetus for the founding of the University Mission which later began to work in East Africa. Livingstone's second great journey — from 1859 to 1864 — was undertaken at the request of the British government who also sponsored it. It involved the exploration of the most important tributaries of the Zambezi and the clarification of missionary, economic and colonising possibilities. The third and final journey took Livingstone to the area around Lake Nyassa for he had long cherished the desire to find the as-yet-unknown source of the Nile. For a long time he was presumed to be dead until Henry Stanley, sent out by the American newspaper *The New York Herald*, found him at Ujiji on October 23, 1871. Although he was sick and reduced to a skeleton, Livingstone refused to accompany Stanley back to Europe and continued to devote himself to his work of exploration until his death on May 1, 1873, at Ilala in what is now Zambia. His loyal African companions buried his heart under a tree and carried his embalmed body hundreds of miles to the east coast. David Livingstone was buried with great honours in Westminster Abbey, London, on April 18, 1874.

"Livingstone was a missionary, a humanist and an explorer. He wanted to make a way for 'Christianity and trade'. He believed in the victory of the Gospel. He declared war on the slave-trade which he frequently encountered in terrible forms. In his view, the only way to reach the traffic in human beings was through control of trade relationships and the development of agriculture. Great pioneer that he was, he not only made roads through the primeval forest, he also paved the way towards turning the world's attention to Africa.

"We have spoken of a Scot; we now turn to a Frenchman. François Coillard was born into a poor peasant family at Asnières near Bourges on July 17, 1834. In response to an inner call he entered the seminary of the Paris Mission in 1856 and only a year later went to South Africa where there was an urgent need for missionaries. In Basutoland he gave 20 years of his life to the establishment of the new mission-station at Leriba. Small of stature, but distinguished by his well-defined features and shining eyes, he generated incomparable energy linked with great humility and selflessness. Thanks to his remarkable flair for languages he learned a number of African languages and laid the basis for a translation of the Bible. He translated and also composed African songs. He saw the formation of native evangelists as one of the most important tasks. In addition he played a decisive role in the establishment of a Church order and of a synod for the Basuto Church. After 20 years, instead of taking his first holiday at home, he complied with a request made by his fellow-workers and set off to investigate the possibilities of missionary work further north. His caravan, made up of three ox-drawn wagons, was exactly two years on the road. Coillard was accompanied by four Basuto evangelists together with their families; this was so that the work could be started straightaway. But the tribal prince of the Banyai responsible for that area forbade them to work there and so they went on into the kingdom of the Barotse. But there too he received the answer, 'not now, later'. As a result he and his wife went back to France in 1880 and there he gave many lectures and collected money for the pioneering work among the Barotse. He returned to Barotseland in 1882 and built the first mission-station in Sefula; this included a school and a room for divine service. The work was hard, and there were many disappointments and confrontations. Many of his companions, including the first mission-doctor, succumbed to the unhealthy climate. Enmities, defamation by his own fellow-workers, the constant battle with the tribal prince who was well-disposed towards him one moment and ill-disposed the next, all these things gave him a lot of trouble, but again and again he fought his way through in faith to trust and hope. In 1891 his wife died; she had been the perfect foil to him and had often helped him to get over his feeling of powerlessness. A year after her death he settled in Leyula, the seat of the king. He was untiring in his missionary work, preaching and teaching, doing pastoral and literary work. At the same time, by introducing ploughs and tools, he tried to improve agriculture and handicraft. He made a second trip to Europe in 1898 and returned to Barotseland with 16 new companions. He set up two new mission-stations and undertook another journey to the Zambezi, this time with a caravan consisting of 80 men, 21 wagons and 330 oxen. But soon his powers began to fail and he died on May 27, 1904. He was buried at Sefula next to his wife.

"From a Frenchman we turn to a German. Johann Gottlieb Christaller was born at Winnenden, Württemberg, on November 17, 1827. He was exceptionally gifted, but his parents were poor and could not afford to pay for his education. He became a town-clerk, but later he entered the seminary of the Basle Mission and in 1853 went to the Gold Coast, present-day Ghana. His unusual gift for languages enabled him to acquire in a remarkably short time a command of the Twi language and later of Ga, a second principal language of the country. He began to work at the college for catechists in Akropong where he was not only a teacher but also a student. In a manner of speaking, he plucked the language from the lips of pupils and of people he met in the street. Each day, in spite of the heat and in spite of mosquitoes, he burned the midnight oil at his desk. He spent only two periods in Ghana — from 1853 to 1858 and 1862 to 1868. For reasons of health he had to remain in Europe from then on, but this did not restrict his tireless language studies. He completed translations, revised works already in print and worked away at dictionaries and textbooks. He was a thoroughly committed missionary and at the same time a born linguist. He made a thorough study of the Twi language, learned its rules, its syntax, its grammar and the significance of pitch. All the time he was comparing it with other African languages of about a hundred of which he is said to have had a pretty good knowledge. The translations he did were closely connected with his work of teaching. The biblical books which were being taught at a given time were translated section by section and checked with scrupulous concern for accuracy with the aid of language teachers and pupils. By 1855 Mark and Luke were ready for printing. Four years later the four Gospels and Acts were printed and in 1871 the complete Bible, which became a popular work. Christaller also composed a hymnbook, translated a catechism, wrote textbooks and collected 3,000 proverbs and many fairy-tales. Philologists paid great tribute to his 671-page Twi dictionary — an encylopaedia — which even today is regarded as a standard work. He was awarded a prize by the French Academy for his comprehensive grammar, he was one of the most important contributors to the then recently established *Zeitschrift für afrikanische Sprachen* and he was in correspondence with all the leading philologists. The fact that in the Ghana of today the native language plays a greater role than it does in many other African countries is to a large extent due to the work of Johann Gottlieb Christaller.

"Finally we turn to the little known but not unimportant figure of Johann Ludwig Krapf, who was born on January 11, 1810 at Derendingen in southern Germany. At 17 years of age he was accepted as a candidate in the seminary of the Basle Mission. However, he left there two years later and went to Tübingen to study theology. In 1837 he went to Abyssinia in the service of the Anglican Church Mission. He learned the language of the Amharas and later that of the Gallas; he began work on a translation of the Bible and made a collection of around 80 rare Ethiopian manuscripts. The University of Tübingen conferred on him an honorary doctorate for these linguistic works. In 1843 he had to leave Abyssinia as did other missionaries. Only after some years did it become clear that by his works on language he had prepared the way for later missionaries. On a fantastic journey he arrived in Zanzibar off the east coast of Africa and then settled at Rabi not far from Mombasa. He eagerly learned Swahili, studied the customs of the people and soon began to translate parts of the Bible. In the company of Johann Rebman, who joined him in 1846 — they became close friends — he explored the interior of the country. Rebman was the first white man to set eyes on the high, snow-covered Mount Kilimanjaro and Krapf, somewhat later, the first to see Mount Kenya. These discoveries made both of them famous, but Krapf often endangered his life. He had been away from Europe for 13 years when he returned there for the first time in 1850. He went back to Africa with five new companions, but these withdrew one after the other and Krapf himself had to return home finally in 1852 because of illness. Later he made only very short trips to Abyssinia and East Africa mainly to accompany and to initiate young missionaries. He died on November 22, 1881 at Korntal near Stuttgart.

"Krapf's missionary work among the Wanika tribe in East Africa bore scarcely any visible fruit. His main claim to fame lay in his explorations and in his linguistic work. He published dictionaries and translations of parts of the Bible in six African languages as well as a Swahili grammar. He wrote down his experiences and the results of his journeys of exploration in a two-volume work entitled *Journeys in East Africa* 1837-1855. But he was not only a geographer and a philologist, he was also an inspired and far-sighted missionary strategist. He had the vision of setting up a chain of mission-stations from Mombasa on the east coast to the Atlantic on the west. He also thought up the idea of an 'Apostles' Way' beginning at Alexandria and going up the Nile; this would consist of twelve spaced-out mission posts each named after one of the Apostles. Like Livingstone he fought against the slave-trade which he came across everywhere, but, unlike the Scot, he was firmly opposed to the foundation of colonies by European powers. He gave wise advice to missionaries. 'It is of the utmost importance', he said, 'that the white man meets the African kings with respect and refrains from all interference in the affairs of the country . . . The missionary must also be grateful for the benefits he receives' ".

* * *

Second Vice-President: "To complete the picture, Fr Albert Thielemeier, a Holy Ghost Father, will speak about the Catholic missions. Fr Thielemeier was head of the German province of his order and is at present one of the Assistants to the Superior General in Rome".

Fr Albert Thielemeier [20]: "Mr President, whenever we think about the ways in which it is possible to travel in Africa today — car, railway, aeroplane — or whenever we look at the mission-stations of the present time, these highly developed cultural centres which served the people for decades until, in the end, the state took over responsibility for the services they had provided, then it is very instructive to cast an eye back to the beginning of this third and latest missionary era and consider the enormous difficulties which those pioneers had to overcome. On the whole, the attitude of the African people to these foreigners was humane and welcoming, but the country and its climate were dreadful. Heroism and supernatural motivation were required to survive the early stages and finally to reach the present point of development. A few spotlights cast on this past may illustrate what I am trying to say.

"In 1842 Rome handed over to the Holy Ghost Fathers the newly erected Vicariate of the Two Guineas, an area stretching more than 5,000 miles from the River Senegal to

[20] This is dealt with more fully in Beckmann's *Die katholische Kirche*, pp. 54-67. Material for the four biographies was provided by representatives of the missionary institutes concerned, viz., Frs Cirillo Tescaroli, J.P. Jordan, J.B. Castanchoa and P.L. Kaufmann.

the River Oranje and for an undefined distance into the interior. The following year, a group consisting of seven priests and three brothers went out there. After only two weeks seven were sick and three died in a short time. One after another they withdrew until there were only two fathers left. The missionaries had written to their founder, Fr Libermann, nine times and hadn't received a single answer. They suspected they had simply been written off because of the foolish mistakes they had made. It was only a year later that a letter arrived; earlier letters from Fr Libermann and their letters to him had never reached their destinations.

"In 1856 Monsignor de Marion Brésillac founded the Lyons Society for African Missions, which was intended to work especially on the west coast of Africa, an area known because of its unhealthy climate as 'the white man's grave'. Brésillac soon found out for himself how accurate this description was. He went with four companions to Sierra Leone and the whole group was wiped out by fever almost immediately after their arrival.

"Cardinal Lavigerie, founder of the White Fathers, sent a group of five from Bagamoyo in East Africa to the area around the Central African lakes. This was in 1878. The leader of the group, Fr Pascal, died of fever, and the remainder reached their destination, Lake Tanganyika, only after a six month march. The following year a second group consisting of twelve men set off. Eight graves marked their route from the coast into the interior. Lavigerie was not put off, and he sent out yet a third group in 1880. On this occasion, speaking in Algiers Cathedral, he declared: 'We, the missionary society and myself, swear that we are prepared to sacrifice the life of every one of our members rather than give up this mission on the Equator'.

"This fearless going out to risk death went on for decades. If we look at the mortality figures for the Holy Ghost Fathers, the following picture emerges. The first twelve missionaries — before 1850 — reached an average

age of 30 years; the 104 between 1850 and 1870 33 years; the 559 between 1870 and 1900 39 years. It is a moving experience to visit a cemetery where the pioneers from that time were buried. In Dar es Salaam, where the German St Ottilien Benedictines began their work in 1888, there lie buried in the oldest cemetery 25 missionaries of both sexes. Of these, ten died during their first year on the missions, seven in their second year, one in his third year, four in their fourth, two in their eighth and only one of them completed ten years! Dozens and hundreds of them died off, but hundreds and thousands came to take their places. Such was the heroic era of the African missions.

"Let me now mention a few characters from the different epochs. I will begin with a woman who really deserves the title of pioneer of the new mission to Africa. Her name is Marie-Anne Javouhey, and she was born at Jallanges in France in 1779. In 1805 she founded the Congregation of the Sisters of St Joseph of Cluny. The original aim of this congregation was to heal the wounds inflicted on the Church by the French Revolution, but when the foundress heard of the needs of the African peoples, her outlook broadened and in 1817 she sent sisters to the East African island of Réunion and in 1819 to Senegal in West Africa. In both places unspeakable difficulties awaited these brave women. The tropical climate and the attendant diseases wore them out; the vast enterprise seemed likely to be too much for their strength. Then the foundress herself, accompanied by six sisters, came to their aid, landing in Senegal in 1822. She saw the desperate plight of the people and the efforts being made by the sisters and she helped them by teaching them better methods of organisation. The same year, 1822, she went on to Sierra Leone to open up a new area of work for her sisters. There she was struck down by that insidious enemy, yellow fever, but she overcame it through the loyal assistance of an African nurse. In 1827 the Negroes of America and of the Antilles Islands benefited from her help and care as did, later, those of the coast of Guyana. Through her work

Mother Javouhey laid the foundations for the devoted work of the sisters in the African apostolate, work which is still going on. She died in 1851 and was beatified in 1950.

"Another figure from the early period was Daniel Comboni. When he was a young student of theology in Verona, Don Angelo Vinco, a missionary in the Sudan, fired him with enthusiasm for the incredibly difficult mission in that country. Don Mazza, who had founded a number of religious institutes in Verona, sent out five priests in 1857 to establish a mission on the White Nile and Comboni was the youngest member of this group. They had hardly reached their destination when they began to die off, one after another. Comboni vowed: 'Either Africa or death'. But his sense of responsibility forbade him to insist on his vow and he returned home because of sickness. Then a group of Franciscans from Styria went to the White Nile and in less than two years 22 of them were dead. The first 20 years produced no results at a cost of 64 lives and it seemed that Central Africa would remain closed to the missionaries. Comboni, however, could not reconcile himself to this and in 1864, while he was praying at St Peter's tomb in Rome, he had a sudden intuition which, when he wrote it down almost without a break, filled 60 pages of paper. It was his 'Plan for the renewal of Africa'. The main idea was to let Africans preach the Gospel in Africa. On the basis of his experience he recognised that methods would have to be changed. Seeing that the climate and the other conditions of life in Central Africa did not permit European missionaries to work there, Comboni gave them the task of setting up and running centres for the formation of Africans in the coastal regions and in other healthier areas. The African catechists, sisters and priests trained in this way would then be able to bring the Gospel to their own people. The European missionaries would work only as pioneers and instructors; everything else was to be left to the Africans. Pope Pius IX studied the plan and encouraged the young Comboni to carry it out. Before going back to Africa, Comboni set out for

Lyons, Paris, Cologne, London, Vienna and Moscow to raise money and personnel for his venture. In Paris he met another pioneer missionary, the Capuchin Cardinal Massaia. The latter, writing to the Roman missionary headquarters, the Congregation for the Propagation of the Faith, described Comboni as 'a heart which carries the burden of Africa'. In addition to his concern for Africa, Comboni was weighed down by concern for his institute. Don Mazza had died in 1865 and his successor, Don Tomba, resigned in the face of various difficulties, including financial ones. It seemed as if everything was collapsing, and so, in 1867, Comboni founded his own institute for the missions in Africa; this was to be followed by an institute for the sisters of Africa (Verona Sisters). He addressed an urgent plea to the First Vatican Council at last to do something courageous for Africa's benefit and not to leave this continent to merchants and colonial powers. In 1872 the Apostolic Vicariate of Central Africa, which stretched from the Red Sea to Benin, was entrusted to his institute. So Comboni again set off on his travels, taking 99 days to reach Khartoum. He tried to organise the vast area, to replace the missionaries who died, to help the people dying of hunger and quietly to put up with the slanderous attacks made on him. Rome's reply to these slanderous attacks was to make the valiant pioneer a bishop, which it did in 1877. In one of his letters Comboni wrote: 'This time I am writing only a few lines because I am broken by fever, by difficulties, by weariness and by heartache. The only way God's work can thrive is at the foot of Calvary. But although I am broken in body, I feel by God's grace fresh in spirit and resolved to suffer everything and to give my life for the redemption of Africa'. The indefatigable standard-bearer of the African missions died in Khartoum on October 10, 1881, at the age of 50. His work continues.

"There are many bishops like Comboni whom we might portray, such as Livinhac, Hirth and Streicher of the White Fathers or Le Roy, Augouard and others of the

Holy Ghost Fathers. One of them, Bishop Joseph Shanahan, we will talk about in some detail. He was born in 1871 in North Tipperary, Ireland, into a respectable farming family in which the true Irish spirit of faith was alive. He was to write later, probably on the basis of his own experience, that a mother's heart is a book in which God's life is revealed to us. His father was a man of vision who used to say that the way to cure Ireland's poverty was not agitation but education. When Joseph Shanahan went to Nigeria in 1902 as a young Holy Ghost missionary, he took this idea of his father's with him. He knew that what counted most in education was not just theoretical instruction but, however loyal one might be to one's cultural heritage, the transformation of the whole man. Three years after his arrival he became Prefect Apostolic of Southern Nigeria and had under him 12 missionaries, seven mission-stations and 1,500 Catholics. Now he was in a position to start carrying out his plans. He was aware the people themselves could never be reached by the system of isolated mission-stations, partly built by ransomed slaves, which had obtained until then. He wanted to push forward into the heart of the country in order to show men the wonders of God's love and teach them the way to a better human life. First of all he convinced the missionaries of the value of the new method. From then on every church became a school and every school the centre of a comprehensive social activity. So there came into being craft schools, domestic science schools, hospitals and nursing schools, model farms and agricultural schools and one should not forget the minor and major seminaries for the training of African priests. In 1932 Shanahan was forced by illness to hand over the reins to someone else, but by then his dream of 30 years earlier had, to a great extent, become a reality. In his missionary territory there were now 110,000 Catholics and 85,000 under instruction. Most important of all something had changed in town and countryside alike. The people had reached a certain standard of living and had become healthily aware of their own identity; they also knew that they owed much of this to the missions. A part of the kingdom of God had become reality here on earth. The sick and finally blind bishop bore witness to this in his deep life of faith. He died in 1943.

"Then there is Fr François Aupiais of the Lyons Missionary Society. He went to Africa in 1903 and spent 23 years there, nearly all of it in Porto Novo, Dahomey, where he was head of the mission-school which at times had over 1,000 pupils. Teachers and pupils alike found in him not only a headmaster but also a friend, an outstanding educator who was conversant with the best methods, was bubbling over with ideas and new plans and was available to anyone who needed him. His concern was not limited to his school; his room became the best known employment agency in the country. Firms and managements vied with each other to get his pupils. A recommendation from Fr Aupiais was of more value than a diploma. One of his main concerns was to get the teachers interested in the cultural riches of the country. These 'educated' people were not infrequently of the opinion that they had nothing to learn from the 'primitives', but Aupiais urged the teachers to observe, to collect, to write down the stories, songs, sayings and usages of their country. In this way they discovered the beauty of their spoken literature and began to be proud of it. In 1925 Aupiais founded the periodical *La reconnaissance africaine*. Many of his former pupils — seminarians, teachers, administrators — discovered to their surprise that they were gifted writers and some of them later became famous. He also tried to arouse a love for their traditional culture in the hearts of the native priests. For him this was a question not of being trendy but of taking evangelisation in its deepest sense, of incarnating the message of Christ into the different cultures, of the unity between God's work of creation and his work of redemption. In 1919 Aupiais became mission-superior and vicar general. Now he devoted himself completely to the care of souls; his thorough knowledge of the native language proved useful to him here. He also tried to make full use of mystery plays and had great success with a nativity play. In 1926, when he went home for a holiday, he took on board with him 30 crates of African art objects. His aim in doing this was to make them available for display and thereby not only raise money for the big church in Porto Novo but also demolish the many preconceived notions about the 'uncivilised' Negroes and produce evidence to prove that contempt for the Africans was based only on ignorance of their cultural riches.

"Unexpectedly his holiday was prolonged to the end of his life. He was appointed head of the Lyons Province and later rector of the seminary for future missionaries. He was able to make only two more trips to Africa: in 1929-1930 when he went with a cameraman to make a film and in the autumn of 1945 when the African regions were allowed for the first time to choose their parliamentary representatives. His loyal followers in Dahomey had pleaded with him to stand for election and, after a great deal of hesitation, he agreed and went out on an election tour. He was in fact elected, but he returned from the tour looking like a man who has suddenly put on ten years. His time had come. A urinary infection brought his life to an abrupt close and he died on December 14, 1945, mourned and honoured by many Africans and Europeans.

"The last person I will mention is someone who was known to many of us here, Fr Jean Louis Goarnisson, M.D. At the age of 80 he retired to the minor seminary in Pabre near Wagadugu in Upper Volta. He was born in France in 1897 and after studying medicine he joined the White Fathers and became a priest. In 1931 he went on the missions in Upper Volta, an area where the people were tormented by two terrible enemies, sleeping-sickness and blindness. The new doctor waged war fiercely and successfully against both these diseases. Untiringly he operated for cataract and trained two White Sisters, who — like him — had studied medicine, as specialists in this field. He then devoted more of his own energy to research because he wanted not only to cure these two most common diseases, he wanted to prevent them and to eradicate them. The fact that sleeping-sickness and blindness occurred together made him suspicious and he was able to establish that one of the agents used to cure sleeping-sickness contained a substance which attacked the optic nerve. After much experimenting he discovered another agent which would cure sleeping-sickness without damaging the optic nerve. This success saved the lives and the sight of thousands of people in the whole of Africa. As well as this, he came across flies which carried on their feet a substance which infected the eyes. Now it is impossible even to think of wiping out flies in Africa, so Goarnisson developed an agent to counteract the substance carried by the flies. In order to put to good use and to pass on his experiences he opened a nursing school, wrote articles about his research and in 1948 published a *Doctor's Guide to Africa* which went through seven impressions. For this work he was awarded honorary doctorates by the Academy of Medicine and the French Academy. In spite of all his medical research he remained a priest and took particular care of the elderly and the blind whom he used to instruct on Sundays. He had a complete command of the Mossi language. Even in his old age he continued to produce fresh audio-visual aids to inform the people about the most important diseases and epidemics. His entire life was spent in the service of his beloved Africans. In 1975, in Paris, R. de Benoist published a book about him; it had the significant title *Docteur Lumière — Doctor Light*.

"Mr President, not all the missionaries are men of this calibre, but certainly all of them have devoted themselves to their task with great courage. In the Catholic missions in Africa there are very many such people even today. Thus there are 2,014 White Fathers, 1,451 Jesuits, 1,435 Holy Ghost Fathers, 890 Capuchins, 726 members of the Lyons Missionary Society, 724 Oblates of Mary Immaculate, 676 Verona Fathers, 590 Franciscans, 561

Scheutveld Missionaries, 527 Brothers of the Christian Schools, and so on. It is my belief that Africa would be much poorer without these men".

* * *

Second Vice-President: "It is not to be unexpected that white people should try to save the honour of the white missionaries, but it is important to know what Africans think about the missionaries and not only those Africans who are opposed to them. The first African to speak in their defence is Professor E.A. Ayandele from the University of Ibadan in Nigeria. He has become known principally because of his indepth study of the influence of the missions on modern Nigeria".

E.A. Ayandele[21]*:* "Mr President, the fact that I have volunteered to speak in defence of the missions does not mean that I have an uncritical respect for the missions and for what they have done. In the book of mine to which you referred I criticised them strongly. Basing myself on files and facts, I found out what Nigerians were thinking about the missionaries between 1842 and 1914. I can only confirm what H.W. Mobley explained in detail in his speech for the prosecution, but I would have to extend what he said, in particular to politics, and prove that the missionaries in their respective regions — French, Belgian and even Irish, American and others in British regions — generally stood in such a relationship to the colonial authorities that they did not regard the rights of the Africans to self-determination as genuine and did not support the national movement when it arose.

"I must point out that the Churches can see this nowadays and have confessed their guilt in this matter. For instance, at the All Africa Churches' Conference held

[21] This speech is based on Ayandele's book, Ki-Zerbo, *Histoire*, pp. 480ff and other sources.

in Alexandria in 1976, the assembled representatives of the Churches declared: 'The storms of history have sometimes made us go astray. We have all too readily left the great Way, Christ, and set out on paths that led nowhere. Often we have spoken against evil only when it was to our advantage to do so. We have often avoided suffering for other people. We have preferred to carry out religious exercises rather than listen to the promptings of the Spirit. Officially we have fought against colonialism and other evils but secretly we have built up again what we had destroyed. We confess that for far too long we have practised a paternalism which is out of date. We have often tolerated exploitation and oppression by foreigners, especially when our fellow-countrymen were the culprits. We have averted our eyes from the injustices in society and have concentrated our efforts on the survival and growth of the Church as an institution. We have so often become a stumbling-block for others. We are truly sorry for these and many other faults and we beg God for his mercy'.

"Mr President, if God does not refuse his mercy to the contrite, how can we do otherwise? Nowadays the missionaries think differently from the way they thought in the past and this is sufficient.

"A further consideration which might help to exonerate the missions as an institution is the fact that the missionary message really had a deep revolutionary effect and that present-day Africa would never have come into being had it not been for this ferment. In saying this, I am referring not only to the mission-schools which were the places where we first learned to think critically and where we first acquired a scientific knowledge of earthly realities, I am referring also to the religious message itself. The doctrine of the descent of all men from Adam, of their creation by God, of the mysterious blood-relationship and equal dignity of all men, the history of the Old Testament with the delivery from Egypt and from enemies, the figure of the Messiah, Jesus Christ, who fearlessly stood up for right before both secular and religious authorities; all this could not fail to have an effect on the awakening self-awareness of Africa.

"The African Christians took these doctrines seriously, and it is no mere coincidence that in Nigeria, and in other places too, the first leaders of the national movement were native church leaders. I agree with E. Bulaji Idowu, a colleague of mine from Ibadan University, when he maintains: 'The Church came to Africa with a prefabricated theology and liturgy and with European usages. But it can also claim justifiably to have been the pioneer and the real creator of the African national movement'.[22] Indirectly and unintentionally, Christianity has, from the very beginning, furthered the religious, cultural and political independence of Africans. In 1888 the first 'African' Church in Nigeria grew out of the Baptist Church. Since that time, independent African Churches have sprung up in such vast numbers that they can scarcely be counted. These Churches appeal exclusively to the Gospel and to those African values which have to be reconciled with it and they represent a radical reform of the African Church. The first two Africans to become bishops of Evangelical Churches in Nigeria — Crowter in 1888 and Johnson in 1900 — were regarded as symbols of the African national movement. Ever since then, most African politicians have come from the mission-schools, not only in the literal sense, but also in the sense that the motivations for their actions in the world have come from the dynamism of the biblical and christian conception of the world. This is true especially of the Evangelical Churches, whereas the Catholic Church has been more intent on forming teachers for its own schools and on forming native priests.

"At the same time Christianity has played a major part in widening the horizon of the old clan-religion and even today is helping to get rid of the dangers of tribal

[22] *The predicament of the Church in Africa* in Baëta's *Christianity*, pp. 417-437 and especially pp. 426ff.

egoism and of a narrow African nationalism. It has confronted Africans with the broad scope of a world-wide religion and, by its doctrine of the brotherhood of all men, has not only lifted up the black men from their former position of humiliation but it has also warned them against taking up a hostile attitude towards the white men.

"As well as these more general and indirect effects of Christianity, there are also concrete cases and records which show that Church leaders have spoken out expressly in favour of the African independence movement. Typical examples are the pastoral letter of the Catholic bishops of Tanganyika in 1953 and the statement made by the Catholic bishops of Madagascar in the same year. The bishops stressed that all peoples have the right to self-determination. 'Man's greatness', they said, 'consists in the fact that he is able to act freely and responsibly. Political freedom is one fundamental form of freedom and responsibility. For this reason the Church recognises the right of people to self-rule as a natural right'. The French colonial press branded this declaration as demagogy and the High Commissioner of Madagascar, Monsieur Barges, returned to it in his new year address when he said, in reply to the address of the bishops: 'It is deplorable that those who are numbered among the spiritual leaders of the population should depart from the teachings of Scripture and in an official pronouncement should incite people to actions which have as their object the overthrow of the present order and the separation from the French community of an integral part of the Republic. One can only wish that this appeal will not be heeded'. In his Christmas address of 1955 Pope Pius XII made himself the interpreter of the rights of the as-yet-unfree peoples and called upon the Western peoples to seek a peaceful solution to the colonial problem in good time. They should not waste their time lamenting the past but should rather meet the problem through constructive work. 'A just and ongoing political freedom should not be denied to these peoples at the appropriate time', the Pope said. One would have to write a whole book if one wanted to bring together all the statements the Churches have made since that time. On the Evangelical side I will mention only the Assemblies held at Uppsala (1968), Bangkok (1973), Lusaka (1974) and Nairobi (1975). Since we have ridiculed the sins of omission committed by the Churches, we should not fail to mention the documents produced by assemblies such as the ones I have mentioned. I must also draw your attention to the courageous bishops and missionaries of the various Churches in Rhodesia and South Africa, who in recent years have stood up quite unequivocally for the rights of the black majority and, as a result, have risked expulsion, imprisonment and even death.

"Nowadays, when nearly all African countries have achieved political independence, the Churches are presented with a new task. They are the critical conscience of society. They alone have the freedom and courage, based on the Gospel and their hope of God's kingdom which is to come, a freedom and courage without which they would not be able to speak out with prophetic voice against all the things which are not good and yet which occur in many countries, things like oppression, arbitrary imprisonment, the murder of political rivals, the inhuman treatment of captives, corruption. If we, as Africans who have won our independence, are reproaching the Churches for their failings, then we must be honest, beat our own breasts and thank the Churches for acting against such abuses and for compelling us, by the pressure of publicity, to be concerned about remedying them.

"The All Africa Churches Conference held in Alexandria, to which I have already referred, added to its declaration the following words: 'In the very moment when the future is breaking into our present, we Christians of Africa have every reason to be happy and confident. Through the continuing work of Christ God is preparing his great way of freedom. We have, therefore, no choice but to continue to fight for the liberation of all men and women and of society as such. We acknowledge the fact that political liberation in Africa and in the Near East is a part of christian liberation. On the other hand, misuse of power and disregard of human rights in many independent African states admonish us to demand a broader understanding of the word "liberation". Seen in this way, "liberation" goes on, and the Churches in Africa have not only the task of baptising children and looking after the sick, they are also inserted into the conflict between poor and rich, between Marxism and Christianity, between democracy and dictatorship. The Churches have much more influence than people think and they should make use of this influence'.

"Mr President, I would like to ask that the Churches be given time and opportunity to continue playing a part in this persistent battle for the liberation of all men and of the whole man".

* * *

Thursday, June 5

First Vice-President: "Today we have the pleasure of listening to one of the most important representatives of African theology, the Reverend John S. Mbiti. An Anglican, he is a professor at Makerere University in Uganda and head of the ecumenical centre in Geneva. He has written several books on the topic under discussion".

John S. Mbiti [23]*:* "Mr President, to begin my remarks I would like to put forward three hypotheses.

"Firstly, the past 100 years of the African missions have been theology-less. No one can disprove this. The same Church which produced the majority of present-day African politicians has produced no real African theologians.

[23] The first part of the speech is based on Mbiti's book, *Eschatology*, pp. 185-191. The remaining material was collected from various other places. The books of the other authors referred to are to be found in the bibliography.

The reason for this is that the missionaries who founded the Churches were not, with few exceptions, theologians. The Church in Africa is founded on faith, but not yet on theology.

"Secondly, the right to and the need for an African theology is generally recognised nowadays. Christianity never existed in a pure state, in a non-incarnate state, and the fact that there is a Western theology, a white theology admits, logically, the possibility of further theologies. The word of God in its Western form has to die in Africa in order to bear fruit. The Gospel is not a dead document, still less is it a rigid system of formulas; it is a message which has to be proclaimed into every cultural setting and confronted with the spirituality it encounters there. Out of this there arises, in addition to faith, theology. This basic demand has been put and described by a great number of authors — for instance E.B. Idowu, H. Sawyerr, T. Tshibangu, A. Shorter, W. Dantine, and also by official documents of the Churches. So the way is open: all we have to do is to walk it! We should not waste any more words demanding the right to create an African theology, but put our intelligence to work creating one. The fact that such a theology does not yet exist is no longer principally a reproach against the white missionaries, it is rather a challenge to us black theologians. It is time that we catch up as quickly as possible on what we have missed.

"Thirdly, we haven't to begin African theology at square one. In recent years a lot has happened which gives one good reason to hope and it is about this that I now want to speak.

"There are now in Africa theological faculties — for Evangelical theology in Yaunde, for Catholic theology in Kinshasa and Abidjan. There are several university institutes of comparative religion and a goodly number of theological colleges, which in many cases are linked with universities. In addition, there is a wide network of schools for catechists and bible-schools, which at the present time are putting across a sound theology. There is a substantial number of professors of theology, most of them Africans nowadays, and already there is an impressive list of printed dissertations written by African candidates for the doctorate in theology. The institutes and faculties I have mentioned publish theological and pastoral periodicals. On the Catholic side there are: *AFER* (Eldoret, Kenya), *Telema* (Kinshasa), *Cahiers des Religions Africaines* (Kinshasa) and on the Evangelical side: the *Ghana Bulletin of Theology* (Lagos), the *Journal of Theology for Southern Africa* (SAAC) published in Orita (Ibadan), the *African Theological Journal* in Mukumura (Tanzania), *Theologia Viatorum* in Turfloop (South Africa) and the *Missionalia* of the South African Missiological Society. There are theological study-weeks and congresses, one example of which is the *Semaines théologiques* of Kinshasa. The Theological Union of the Third World was established recently and it held its first meeting in Dar es Salaam in August 1976. At grass-roots level — and this is perhaps more important than the heights of theology — there is taking place a renewal of the liturgy. This is portrayed, for instance, in books by B. Luykx and B. Bürki and it can be seen nowadays in many African countries where the liturgy is, in the fullest sense of the word 'celebrated', where the community spends two to four hours in prayer, singing, listening to the Word of God and talking about it. This is where, quietly and in an unassuming manner, African theology is coming into being.

"Now all this contains a potential of tremendous richness. It is true that, as yet, we have no *Summa* of African theology, but after the long drought of traditional theology rain has fallen on the fields and everywhere things are beginning to sprout and to blossom. Books such as those of H. Bürkle, Th. Sundermayer, H.J. Becken, J.H. Cone, V. Mulago and some of my own books together with magazine articles give some indication of this theological springtime.

"We are, then, at the beginning of a process the results of which we cannot yet in any way foretell. Some people are afraid of it, others see in it the working of God's Spirit who at last is making his Church, which until now has been a Western Church, into a world Church. Until the present time, it was really only one continent which made theology for the other five and even in this one continent it was really only a few men who created scholastic theology, which was then repeated for centuries. But from now on all six continents are going to make theology and this will be the work not only of a few professors, it will take place also at the grass-roots of the Church. From this movement we can expect a theological explosion, an unequalled theological wealth. It will no longer be a question of a theology of the classroom but of a theology of life, of a genuine dialogue between men who believe in the Gospel and in the Lord Jesus Christ; between men who believe in 'their' god and who at the same time know that there is only one God, the God and Father of all men; between men who no longer believe in God at all, secularised men and Marxists who, in spite of being such, cannot shake off the ultimate questions about the meaning of life; between men who no longer hope only for a heaven but who even now want to make whole their own life and that of all humanity.

"In classical missiology the term 'adaptation' or 'accommodation' was used. This term was based on the notion that the whole christian ethos as it had been formed in 2,000 years of Western Church history could be brought to Africa and that only certain areas, for example, music and church decoration, would need to be adapted to the prevailing circumstances. Nowadays the term 'incarnation' is used, and the meaning of this term is that the essence of the Gospel should be brought to Africa and should take shape, should take flesh in African culture and make its history in Africa. I would like to demand a third stage — 'interpretation'. This notion does not exclude that of 'incarnation' but presumes it and goes beyond it. When one speaks of 'interpretation' one means that one no longer wants only to sit in a church and meditate on the Gospel together with believers; one wants to interpret in the light of the Gospel the whole of reality, even that outside the Church, and to speak the word of salvation over the whole world and the whole human race.

"We theologians, then, are no longer involved only in ecumenical dialogue within the Churches, we are also involved in a three-cornered dialogue — with traditional African religion, with Islam and with the secularised Marxist world. This dialogue can no longer be conducted only in the form of discussions, it needs also a mutual sharing of religious experience. Only when one has this, is one in a position to judge others. This is something fascinating for us. We are not frightened of this dialogue, for if Christ is with us, who can be against us? We do not, however, expect that in this dialogue there will be victors and vanquished, but we do expect that all parties will be honest with themselves and with each other in all they think and say. In this way we will continually come closer to one another. It is the task of theology in Africa to conduct this dialogue in Africa and the fruit of this dialogue will be African theology which, in its turn, will enrich world theology.

"Mr President, one should not chalk up against the missionaries the fact that, in the past, for reasons connected with the age in which they lived, they did not conduct this dialogue sufficiently; one should be grateful to them for the fact that nowadays they urge us on to this dialogue and help us in conducting it".

* * *

First Vice-President: "You are now going to hear Fr Waly Neven, a Belgian member of the White Fathers and Secretary of the R.C.A. (Rencontre de Collaboration Africaine), a body which links the Council of the African

Episcopal Conferences with the Union of Superiors General in Rome".

Waly Neven[24]: "Mr President, the R.C.A. is very concerned that African priests and missionaries from other Churches should work well together. On behalf of this body I have to tell you about the change which has taken place in the relationship between these two groups of priests in the Catholic Church.

"Anyone who surveys the century or more of modern missionary history knows that each of the various missionary institutes had, in fact, according to the so-called *jus commissionis,* its 'own' missions, that is to say, missionary territories allotted to it by Rome. In its own territories a missionary institute had full responsibility and its members devoted all their energies to the proclamation of the Gospel and the establishment of the Church. These old-time missionaries were in a class of their own; they were hard men and women who defied all difficulties, strong personalities who, in the face of the many needs of the Africa of their day, took initiatives without many if's and but's. They knew intuitively what was the right course to follow. They made use of the prestige which, as white people, they enjoyed in those days. They regarded dialogue as a luxury and the seeking of advice as a waste of time and energy. They were realistic and pragmatic, and without a doubt they created something.

"In the meantime, however, things have changed. The Africans, not least thanks to the work of those missionaries, have become aware of their own identity as a people and as a Church. Over the years, nearly all the Apostolic Vicariates — a typical institution of a missionary Church — have become dioceses and the Second Vatican Council

[24] The text was compiled by Fr Waly Neven and is based substantially on the document *Evangelisierung in der Mitverantwortung,* published in *Actes de la quatrième Assemblée générale du Symposium,* pp. 181-187, and on a similar document of the same name published by the African bishops at the Synod of 1974.

has developed the theology of the local Church. As a result the custom of entrusting an area to a missionary order was abandoned in 1969. All of a sudden the missionaries are expected to play a different role. From being independent founders of Churches, they have to become servants of the local Church; from being people in authority, they have to become men of dialogue, listeners and, willy-nilly, even men of obedience. My confrère, Fr Bernard Joinet, put this very bluntly when he wrote: 'For myself, I am convinced that when the Christians of Africa speak, the Churches of the West will tremble'. It may well be that the missionaries will tremble even more.

"It is true that, theoretically, one knew from the very beginning that at some future time Africa would have to be evangelised by Africans but, in practice, people became fully conscious of this only when Pope Paul VI during his visit to Uganda in 1967, almost shocked them by uttering the following brave words: 'Our presence among you should have no other purpose than to give recognition to your full maturity. From now on you Africans are your own missionaries. The Church of Christ is really implanted in your blessed soil'. Naturally, he went on to say immediately: 'The help of fellow-workers coming from other Churches is still necessary for you today. Accept this help with love and reverence and fit it in wisely into your pastoral work'.

"The African bishops are aware that the majority of their priests and sisters still come from the missionary institutes and that, for the time being, they cannot do without this help. These institutes have at their disposal not only good helpers but also a great number of specialists. In order to secure and make better use of this treasure, the R.C.A. was founded to link together the African bishops and the Superiors General of the various orders and congregations. One of the first documents to be produced by the R.C.A., at Accra in 1974, deals with the new position of the foreign missionaries in the African Church.

"Even though the majority of missionaries were psychologically successful in adapting to this new situation and retreating to a position of secondary importance, this changing of the guard (if one may use that expression) is not taking place completely smoothly and this is understandable. There arose a sense of discomfort which has not disappeared entirely even today and it varies in strength from one country to another. The African priests feel, as it were, that they have their backs against the wall pressed by the overwhelming weight of the white missionaries who usually have louder voices, more money and more stubborn ideas. Either secretly or openly they wish that the missionaries would withdraw as the Evangelical Churches suggested when they put forward the idea of a moratorium. For their part, the missionaries themselves no longer feel at ease. They ask themselves whether they are simply tolerated rather than wanted and whether it would not be better, therefore, to quit the arena so as to leave the Africans to manage their own affairs alone. There developed what one might call a 'theology of self-withdrawal'.

"What is at issue here is primarily a problem of the clergy rather than of the people. Generally speaking, the people have nothing against the missionaries, quite the contrary. We are faced with the psychological situation that many African priests feel that they are not yet accepted and many missionaries feel that they are no longer accepted; as a result, both groups are suffering a kind of frustration. The problem can be resolved only on the basis of mutual understanding and of supernatural rather than purely natural reaction. Anyone looking at the matter objectively cannot fail to see that the right way to deal with this is not by making a break but by a systematic and organic replacement. The African bishops, who bear the responsibility for their Churches, know that they still need the missionaries. This is why they are worried by this mood of crisis, this defeatism, this spirit of withdrawal on the part of the missionaries. In their pronouncements they have stressed repeatedly that what is at issue is not that the missionaries should retire from the missions but that they should adapt themselves to the new situation. Hence, in the document published in Accra in 1974 to which I have already referred and which one might describe as the Magna Carta of missionary cooperation, the following points are made among others.

(a) The missionary is a part of the local Church. He is not an 'alien' but a fellow-worker having a full share of responsibility, not only a person who does a job or an expert whose advice one asks. However, he is not so much an 'envoy' (a 'missionarius'), who comes here without being invited and who spends a lifetime here, as a 'guest' who stays here as long as he is needed.

(b) On the other hand, the missionary should never forget that, no matter how much he adapts to the mentality and life-style of the local Church, he comes from a culturally and sociologically different milieu. There is no need for him to conceal this fact; on the contrary, he should bring precisely this different background of his to the local Church as an enrichment, but offering it rather than forcing it and without regarding 'his' theology as the only correct one. He should introduce his background into the dialogue tactfully and skilfully, not forgetting that, in the end, it is the Africans themselves who have to introduce Christianity into African culture and make it take flesh there.

(c) The missionary should be prepared to play less of the competent organiser and manager than hitherto and he should accept humbly that African characteristics, which do not always appeal to foreigners, are perhaps, in the long run, more effective and more profound. He should take initiative in an unpretentious way and not adopt a schoolmasterly attitude towards the African clergy.

(d) The missionary should, as a normal thing, put up

with a degree of psychological uncertainty. He cannot simply ignore questions such as: how long is one going to be needed? or wanted? by the Church? by the government? What is the political, economic and ecclesiastical future of this country? Such questions — and the likelihood of no answer to them — can be a burden, but risk and uncertainty were from the very beginning a part of missionary existence.

(e) In spite of everything, the missionary should regard the future of Africa with optimism and should spread this optimism in his own country. He should endeavour to see the positive aspects rather than the defects because criticism and sarcasm cripple whereas confidence and joy awaken those forces which the African Church needs.

(f) Finally, the missionary should know that the main goal of his work is to build up an African Church, a Church which can govern itself, which can pay for itself and which can propagate itself. So that it can do all this, the missionary has to form for it a fully competent African staff. Having done this, the missionary will, in the long run, render himself superfluous, which is what is meant by his 'dying and becoming', his service as a John the Baptist.

"These considerations have been discussed, deepened, absorbed and translated into action at many conferences and at all levels, in a constant interchange from bottom to top, from the mission-stations to the Union of Superiors General and back again. One cannot say that the feeling of discomfort has disappeared everywhere, but it has certainly diminished and will diminish still further. Of course, life on this earth can never be entirely free from friction. There can be friction not only between the African clergy and the missionaries but also within these two groups; this is normal and human. So then, the Catholic bishops of Africa do not want to break off their relations with the older Churches but they do want to change their character. Hence it is that the notion of 'missions' which corresponded to the old idea of entrusting a territory to a foreign organisation and was an expression of guardianship and dependence, is giving way to the expression 'communion', that is, fellowship between the Churches such as existed in the first christian centuries and, it is to be hoped, will exist always.

"And so not only the many concrete forms of service the missionaries have to render the African Church become clear, their new function does too: the missionaries are becoming ambassadors between the Churches. No longer have they simply to bring to Africa from the older Churches what Africa needs, they also have to bring back to their own, older, Churches from Africa what these Churches need. No Church is ever completely sufficient to itself and if it ever conceived the idea that it was, it would indeed be conceited. All the Churches need one another. It can be only of benefit to the Churches of the North Atlantic if they not only become aware of the spontaneity in the liturgy, of the types of communities which are alive even though they have no priest, and of the missionary dynamism of the African Church, but also learn something from all this for their own pastoral situation. In the past we have always given and taught; now we should be ready humbly to receive and to learn. The older Churches, so weary and so resigned as they are, can rejuvenate themselves. This is how a mutual penetration, a living exchange of pastoral experiences between the Churches comes about. This is how from the many local Churches there comes into being one universal Church — if one regards the Church as a living fellowship in one faith and one love rather than as a juridical structure. Seen in this light and under these conditions, there will continue to be a place in Africa for young missionaries who want to devote the best part of their lives to a sister-Church. In like manner Asian and African priests will be welcome in the European

Churches if they come there with a truly priestly disposition.

"Mr President, I believe that it would go against the interests of the African Church — and also against the concept of the Church as a whole — if one tried to put an arbitrary stop to this interchange between the Churches. Let us allow life to take its course and find its own solutions".

* * *

First Vice-President: "We are now going to hear from representatives of the two top-ranking organisations of the Churches in Africa. The Reverend Joseph Osei, representing the Catholic Church, is Secretary General of the Council of the Episcopal Conferences of Africa and Madagascar based in Accra".

Joseph Osei [25]*:* "Mr President, I stand before you as an African priest — there are more than five thousand of us — but I stand here not to accuse the missionaries, as has become the fashion in certain circles; no, I am here to accuse us African priests and African Christians as Cardinal Paul Zoungrana did in the homily he delivered at the Council of Episcopal Conferences in Rome in 1975. As President of this Council he confessed publicly that we too had our faults and our sins, that we, by our deeds and our words, had all too often been an obstacle to God's work of salvation and that all we had to look to was God's mercy and reconciliation in the Church.

"Now if this attitude is an honest one, and if we can see the beam in our own eye, then we cannot condemn

[25] The historical part has been compiled from various sources. The newer angles are ideas which Cardinal Paul Zoungrana has repeatedly expressed, for instance in his talk at the 4th Council of African Bishops in Rome in 1975. Cf. *Actes*, pp. 191-193. One might refer also to Bishop P. Sarpung's contribution, *Indigénisation*, op. cit., pp. 105-113, and Archbishop B. Gantin's *Evangelizzare oggi in Africa*, in *Settimana di Studi missionari*, pp. 11-37.

others because of the splinter in their eyes. Certainly the course of history has been a peculiar one. The Roman Congregation for the missions, which used to be called the Congregation for the Propagation of the Faith and is now known as the Congregation for the Evangelisation of Peoples, was founded in 1622. From the very beginning it urged missionaries not to suppress native culture and to regard the formation of a native clergy as their principal task. Indeed, even as early as the 16th century there were native priests in the Congo, as well as a native bishop, Don Henry, who was ordained bishop on May 5, 1518. This ideal of forming a native clergy was, however, abandoned because of some rather negative experiences and because of increasing racial arrogance on the part of white people; it was revived only at the beginning of this century. Naturally enough, there are still great difficulties to be faced in this matter. With reference to the earliest attempts to form a native clergy in Kisubi, Uganda, in the years from 1892 to 1900, we are told that around 400 boys began their studies for the priesthood but only four of these were ordained. Most of them gave up because they felt it was impossible for such as them to become priests. And yet it has become possible!

"For a long time the question was asked whether it was not appropriate to open up an easier way to the priesthood for Africans, to give them a basic training which would just enable them to carry out priestly functions. Rome, however, was firmly opposed to this idea which, if it were adopted, would produce a second-class clergy who would always be inferior to the white missionaries and would thus be a kind of clerical proletariate. This was something to be avoided at all costs if the African Church was ever to stand on its own feet. Pope Benedict XV in his Encyclical *Maximum Illud* of 1919 put the final seal on this line of approach. After recommending missionary bishops to train native priests, he went on: 'It is, however, necessary to give native priests a good formation. This formation must be complete and rounded off in all its aspects like the formation given to our priests. The native priests must be trained not only to the extent that they can relieve the foreign missionaries of certain tasks but so that they will be equal to all the tasks of a priest and able, at some time in the future, to take over completely as leaders of their people'. This far-seeing directive was observed and the result is that today we have an African clergy who in no way fall behind the missionaries and who can move among the educated African lay élite without feeling inferior.

"At the present time there are in Africa 44 well-established seminaries with 3,811 students. In 1975 260 Africans were ordained to the priesthood. This number is by no means sufficient, but there is a hope that it will increase in the future since in some countries the seminaries have more candidates than they can take. 1939 marked the episcopal ordination of the first African bishop of modern times, Joseph Kiwanuka of Masaka in Uganda. The second followed after an interval of thirteen years, but then there began an uninterrupted series of appointments with the result that on September 1, 1974, there were 155 African bishops in 301 dioceses south of the Sahara. It will take perhaps 20 years until the generation of white missionary bishops has died out. So then, the leaders and other holders of positions of responsibility in the African Church are now Africans. At the last meeting of the Council of the African Episcopal Conferences in 1975, out of 46 delegates only six were white and of these three came from South Africa and two from North Africa. Moreover, at the present time Africa has seven black cardinals, and considering that it has only 40 million Catholics, it is in a privileged position with reference to other countries.

"In the middle ranks, that is, among the priests, the proportions are not so encouraging. There are 11,500 foreign missionaries but only 5,000 African priests. We cannot yet manage without the missionaries and we cannot yet replace them. The Church in Africa at the present time acquires one and half million Catholics annually but only

250 new priests. Under these circumstances it would be a crime against the Church to want to release the missionaries. We are doing all within our power to further priestly vocations, to encourage the laity to accept more responsibility, to develop various forms of service. But all this takes time. We have to walk, not fly, along the road to a fully African Church.

"Again, in the name of Cardinal Zoungrana, I have to thank the Churches of Europe and America for sending us so many of their best sons and daughters as missionaries. We hope that the example given by and the impulse generated by these professional missionaries will make our African Church a missionary Church too.

"It is true that our problems are not confined to questions of personnel. Until the present we have had in Africa a Christianity which was alien to us and which alienated us. Both the texts and the tunes of the hymns were foreign to us and the Gospel message was reduced to abstract catechism formulas. Morality was taught on the implicit assumption that Africans hadn't the least inkling of good behaviour. Baptised Africans could not help getting the impression that their day-to-day life as Africans was irreconcilable with Christianity. Our task for the future is to incarnate Christianity, to africanise it. All the documents of the Second Vatican Council as well as *Africae terrarum* (1967) and *Evangelii nuntiandi* (1975) give us the right to do this. We must only have the courage to act accordingly, even though isolated lower and higher authorities within the Church still equate the unity of the Church with uniformity. It is more than a question of translating the Gospel from foreign languages into our African languages; we have also to transpose it into our African ethos, bring face to face with it our cultural and religious tradition, the present and future problems of our economic and political development, the claims of our poor and of our young people, and we have to give a christian-African answer to men seeking for a better and more meaningful life. We are convinced that the Gospel has a message for the university professor and for the illiterate fisherman, for the dedicated nurse and for the corrupt official. Everyone should be affected by it and, from then on, direct their lives towards the kingdom of God.

"We are only at the beginning of this endeavour. The African Church is still young, its history is only just beginning and the future lies before us. Evangelisation is a dynamic commission and one which looks to the future. Our Churches, therefore, and the missionaries who serve them, remain optimistic not only because of the singular development which the evangelisation of Africa has undergone in past decades but also because of — and precisely because of — the difficulties, the criticisms and the conflicts we are having to meet and deal with.

"Nearly 2,000 years ago, certain forces tried to wipe out the as-yet young Church on the grounds that it was destroying their tradition. And then a Pharisee named Gamaliel, a man held in high esteem by all the people, stood up in the Council of the Jews and gave his colleagues this advice: 'Keep away from these men and let them alone; for if this plan or this undertaking is of men, it will fail; but if it is of God, you will not be able to overthrow them. You might even be found opposing God' (Ac 5:38-40 RSV). Mr President, I credit you and your council with wisdom like that".

* * *

First Vice-President: "Our next speaker is the Reverend Burgess Carr from Liberia. He is Secretary General of the Protestant All Africa Churches Conference based in Nairobi".

Burgess Carr[26]*:* "Mr President, what is taking place

[26] The text is taken almost verbatim from Canon Burgess Carr's address at the Fourth Council Meeting of the African Episcopal Conferences held in Rome in 1975. Cf. *Actes*, pp. 201-204.

at the highest level in the relations between the Vatican and the World Council of Churches in Geneva, relations which have changed for the better, is being reflected in the relations between the two top-ranking christian institutions in Africa, the Catholic Council of the Episcopal Conferences of Africa and Madagascar and the Protestant All Africa Churches Conference.

"We cannot deny that there have been faults and failings in the past, but the question at issue is whether the institution known as the missions should be allowed to remain in Africa or whether it should be wiped out. This institution, therefore, must be judged on the basis of what it is like today and what it will probably be like tomorrow rather than on what historians can tell us about what it was like in the past. From my own experience I can testify that I am bound by ties of friendship to many representatives of the Catholic Church, but also that the official relations between our two organisations have really undergone a radical change for the better over the years and that they are still improving. This is the case not only over a wider area and at top-level but also in most countries and regions. In at least six countries, viz., the Congo, Gambia, Lesotho, Swaziland, the Sudan and Uganda, there is a single national Council of Churches, that is, of all the Churches. In many other countries two separate Councils work very closely together, for instance, in the fields of education, religious instruction, the health service, the development of the country, the formation of the laity, pastoral work in the towns, the mass-media, Bible translation, the defence of human rights — in other words, all along the line. If one wanted to give a detailed picture, one would have to mention hundreds of activities. At regional level — for example, in the East African countries — we have undertaken joint investigations into the question of evangelisation, into the problems of the christian family, into joint training courses for pastoral work in the towns. Even in our joint concern about the content of the faith we should proclaim to the men of today and the method of proclaiming it we can count on each other.

"Certainly there are things which still divide us and we may not overlook this fact, but the things which unite us in friendship and in common loyalty to Jesus Christ carry much more importance and weight. Based as they are on the past, our ways are parallel but separate. Contemporary history is, however, bringing us more and more together in a common loyalty to our common Lord and for this we thank God.

"At the present time our continent is in labour and from these pains something new will come forth, something great. After two decades of political independence and, at the same time, of dependence, we are awakening to ourselves. We are becoming aware of our geographical position in the world. Africa is no longer a sleeping giant, it has begun to stir, and the other countries will have to take us into account. They are taking an interest in our continent and no longer only in its mountains and lakes, its nature reserves and its mineral resources; they are also, at long last, taking an interest in the African mentality. They are discovering that, in Africa, man occupies the central place and that Africa has a decisive contribution to make towards humanising a world dominated by technology.

"Those of us who have been called by God to lead the Churches of Africa feel the obligation, today more than ever before, to be true Africans and, at the same time, true Christians. We are caught, so to speak, in the magnetic field between the universal and the particular. Both poles have a deep influence on our existence but under both these aspects we have the same objective to realise, viz., loyalty to Christ. We cannot allow his name to become a stumbling-block because of our apparent disobedience. On the contrary, all of us must, in dedication, service, adoration and praise enrich the common brotherhood which unites us around his name. It is my belief that in this way we are living out the deepest meaning of the catholicity of the Church.

"Reflections of this nature determine nowadays the programmes of all our Churches in Africa in the fields of evangelisation, theological research, human development and justice for all. As a matter of course we invite one another to our meetings and we notice time and again that we are all facing the same problems and that we are all being challenged by the same situations. The question at issue is: What does it mean to be the Church of Christ in the Africa of today? We have adopted styles of life, theological systems, forms of organisation and liturgical practices which were the self-expression of Churches in other parts of the world. We have tried all these out for a long time and we have had to recognise in the end that they are an obstacle to our genuine witness to Christ, that they alienate our minds and become for us a burden rather than a help. Certainly we don't want to throw out the baby with the bath-water. We love Christ, but we have to find ways and means of making him and his message take flesh in Africa. Our religion is an incarnational religion, but for far too long we have made its values spiritual and abstract; we must make them concrete again. What we have to do is to show by our lives and not by our words that we love Christ and belong to him, that we are converted men, new men. Only in this way can we convert others to Christ and give all men hope that the kingdom of God is on the way.

"At this hour when a new era is coming to birth, we have to speak as prophets. We have to interpret this new era and create hope for the future. Our witness will be effective in the measure in which we do this together and we will grow ever closer together. In spite of all our joy in our discovery of each other and in the esteem in which we hold each other, we are still saddened by the fact that, for historical reasons, when dealing with common problems and meeting common challenges, we still retain separate structures and pursue the same goal along separate paths. Just as we judge past decades from the standpoint of the present, and to that extent condemn them, in the same way future generations will make judgements about us unless we acquire the courage to become more united, to develop a joint strategy and to carry out our mission in Africa together.

"In this speech my aim has been, at the highest level and before the whole of Africa, to cast a glance not only backwards but, above all, forwards and to express my hope, indeed my firm conviction, that in the very near future, the Holy Spirit will lead us to an even more firm solidarity, an even more visible unity.

"Mr President, give us the time we need. We will grow together even more and, reversing the past, will become, not a leaven of division but a leaven of unity and all the peoples of Africa will see the salvation of God".

* * *

Friday, June 5

The President: "As a fitting conclusion to this series of speeches we are going to listen today to Julius Nyerere. There is really no need for me to introduce him to you. As you know, he was the founder of the T.A.N.U., the National Party of Tanzania, and subsequently became the first President of that country. He did not stand for election in 1979 and since then he has been living in a Ujamaa village as a 'mzee', that is, an 'elder', with all the honours customarily paid to people of that status. He believed that the best way he could serve his country (I would like to add — 'and all Africans') was by leading the life of an ordinary citizen and worker. Had he still been President of his country he would not have been able to speak here, because the council of elders would not have wanted to be put under pressure by a man having political power. But we will listen attentively to what he has to say to us now as a citizen. Mr Nyerere, you may now address us".

J. Nyerere [27]: "Mr President, I am speaking here as an African and as a Christian. In stating this, I do not mean that every African must be a Christian; I do mean, however, that an African can be a Christian without ceasing to be a good African. My idea of God — and hence also of man, who is made in his image and likeness — is so big that I would not presume to judge others. Every man, in his freedom, shares in the mystery of God's absolute freedom. Hence every man can, according to the strength of his convictions and in his own way, reach heaven in so far as he is simply a good man. I found my way into the Catholic Church when I was 20 years old and I would not have wished things to have worked out differently.

"I have always, even when I had to take into account political considerations, reserved for myself the freedom to say what was in my heart and in my mind. Because of this I have not infrequently given offence to those who thought differently. But if everyone thought the same way, there would be no more conversation, no more progress in thought would be made, and life would become tedious. In open exchange thoughts are developed, corrected, confirmed. Some of the things I did caused shock in ecclesiastical circles at first; for instance, when I showed special favour to the Muslims who had previously been neglected in the educational system; when I put forward my socialistically-slanted programme; when I brought the Chinese into the country, taxed the missions and took over the mission-schools for the state. Since then, all these things have not only become routine, they have proved themselves to be good.

"It is precisely because I am a Christian that I considered it my task to point out to the Churches their correct place. During the colonial period they had become

[27] The text is based substantially on various addresses made by Nyerere, especially on his address to the Maryknoll Congress entitled *The Church and society*; this address is printed in his book, *Freedom and Development*, pp. 212-228. It is based also on various conversations he has had with the Tanzanian bishops.

a state within a state. Their activity in schools and hospitals, an activity which without a doubt was meritorious, was given a too clerical character, it was too closely orientated to the Church. The Churches saw in their activity not so much a selfless service of mankind as a means to an end, that of their own expansion. They even tried to rope the state into their service by demanding, for instance, that the christian concept of marriage should be protected by law. Now all this had to change and it has changed. From the beginning I have supported the view that Church and State should not hold each other's stirrup as they have done in Europe since the Middle Ages. Church and State live and work on different levels but they should, of course, recognise each other's functions. The socialist state is lay, areligious; it is concerned not with religion but with man's earthly well-being. But man as man can be religious and in my view it is good that he sees in his life a final, transcendental meaning. The state has only the task of guaranteeing full freedom of religious belief and worship — as long, of course, as this doesn't go against public order — to people as individuals and as groups, which latter are called Churches or religious communities. This view also has now become common currency especially as Article 18 of the Human Rights Declaration of 1948 recognises freedom of conscience and religion as one of the fundamental rights of man.

"When I make a distinction between the functions of the Church and those of the State, I do not in any way intend to say that the Churches and religions should be concerned only with man's eternal life and show no interest in his earthly well-being on the grounds that this is the responsibility of the state. On the contrary, I am of the opinion that the religions have to give man, precisely on the basis of their specific way of looking at things, effective motivations for transforming this so imperfect world into a free and better world. We Christians say that man is created in God's image: this thought has always affected me and moved me deeply. Now I simply refuse to imagine

God as poor and stupid, confused and timid, depressed and ragged. I cannot, in consequence, resign myself to the fact that the vast majority of those who are made in the image of God in no sense live like this. Man should have mastery over himself and over the conditions of his life. But in fact, in the circumstances of the present day, we are not God's creatures and his children, we are slaves and creatures of stronger and brutal men.

"This is why the Churches and their members must do all they can to help men to an existence worthy of man and of God. There can be no element of holiness in enforced poverty. It may well be that saints can live in slums, but that doesn't mean we should preserve slums as nurseries for saints! In the conditions of life in the slums most people — and, after all, not everyone is a saint — become useless to themselves, to their families and to the nation. Now this cannot be God's intention regarding man.

"I am not saying that the Churches should carry on a lot of works independently as they did in the past when the state was not in a position to care for the earthly well-being of the citizens. Nowadays Church people should no longer work *for* the people, they should work *with* the people. They have to give the people self-confidence, trust, joy, awareness of their own dignity, the will to work and a sense of responsibility. The Church people should be right in the thick of things and set to work. In this way christian motivations become concrete, exemplary, effective. Development consists not so much in constructing projects as in transforming man, in mobilising the powers which he has but which are impeded. This work of mobilisation is the decisive contribution the Churches can make. The people listen to churchmen because they have access to the grass-roots. They are all over the place and every Sunday millions of Africans sit at their feet. True worship, worship pleasing God, means not only praying heavenwards but also loosing the chains of injustice, bursting the bonds of slavery, breaking every kind of yoke, sharing one's bread with the hungry, letting the dawn of a better day break, as the prophet Isaiah proclaimed. I have said time and again to the bishops and other Church leaders: 'If you do not use your influence to help me, then my socialistically-conceived policy is pie in the sky'. If the Churches do not take our poverty seriously and do not help to overcome it from within, then the Churches, as far as we are concerned, no longer exist, they lose all significance. And others who do not believe in God will come, will build a better world for tomorrow and will make our hope in God unworthy of credit.

"Now I don't go around waving Communism about as a threat; on the contrary, I take Communists very seriously because they identify themselves with the poor. Something good doesn't become bad because it is done by Communists and, conversely, something bad doesn't become good because it is done by Christians; but I do find it absurd that Christians do not stand up for the poor more than the Communists do. This is why I have said repeatedly to Church leaders that they should not be fighting Communists but rather building a society which doesn't need Communism. The Churches have an unheard-of chance: I only hope they will see it and make use of it.

"I come now to the real heart of the problem here under discussion, the relationship between the African Church and the 'expatriates', the foreign missionaries. The first comment I would like to make is that this manner of speaking is not appropriate in the Church. A state can speak of 'expatriates', foreigners, people who are not citizens of that state. But in the christian Churches there are neither Greeks nor barbarians, freemen nor slaves, foreigners nor natives. No matter where a priest or a pastor proclaims the word of God and performs his ministry, in that place are his love, his Church, his homeland. It is precisely Christianity which has to help us overcome the tribal way of thinking and to replace the many tribal deities by the one God and Father of all men. Speaking personally, over the past 40 years I have got to know and to esteem many missionaries, men and women, Catholic and Protestant. They have been close to me, they have given me personal and political support and I owe them an undying debt of gratitude. I have always admired the sisters more than anyone else. In their dedication they remain an example for all our citizens. The last thing in the world I would want would be to plead for the severing of these connections, for the expulsion of the missionaries. The truth is, we cannot place colonialism and the missions on the same footing and make an end of them both in the same way.

"Nevertheless I believe that, particularly in the Catholic Church, there is still a disproportion in the relative numbers of African and white priests and sisters. At the very beginning of independence I put forward a programme for my country, setting as a target that by 1980 we would have enough teachers and other specialists of our own. We have gone a long way towards reaching that target. The Catholic Church has not kept sufficiently in step with this rhythm of africanisation. It is true that practically all the key positions have been given to Africans and this is the main thing. But we still need missionaries for certain specialised tasks. We welcome them, but they must understand that their principal task is to form native trained personnel and thus make themselves superfluous in the long-term. In this way, although the world Church is universal, here in Africa the Church will become, in the full sense of the word, an African local Church because, in the last resort, we Africans bear the responsibility for our Church in Africa ourselves. No one can, and no one should — even with the best of intentions — take this responsibility from us. The handing-over of responsibility from the Europeans to ourselves should not be carried out by force but should take place as an organic process of development. God has often turned forceful interventions in the history of salvation to good account, but the men responsible for such interventions are not without guilt.

"My view then is that for a long time to come there will be place for a certain number of missionaries of both sexes. The people trust them and respect them; they look upon them as symbols of justice, progress, hope, of affiliation to a world-wide Church. We have to admit in all honesty that even in our states a too-speedy africanisation has shown itself not to be of benefit to the people. As well as this, nowadays the world and mankind are becoming more and more one. In France, Great Britain, the United States of America and elsewhere scores of Africans and Asians have taken up permanent residence; this leaves out of account those who are studying in these countries for some years and those holding diplomatic posts. Why then shouldn't Europeans and Americans have the right of domicile in Africa, especially those of them who want to serve Africa unselfishly? In my view, a healthy mixture of races and people can only profit all parties concerned and will be characteristic of the world of the future.

"Nowadays, the religions more than anyone else have the function of link-men. For too long they divided men. Thank God we have now gone beyond this stage. Religious people should feel at home everywhere. I see one of the most promising signs of the times in the opening-out and the meeting between Churches and religious such as we have experienced in recent years. I am, therefore, confident and I believe that the religions have an irreplaceable service to offer man in all his dimensions until the end of time.

"Mr President, in introducing me you stressed that my words are in no sense to be understood as a form of pressure on the council of elders. But I am aware of my obligations to Africa and to Africans and I believe I have a duty to express my conviction that the missions have changed greatly in recent times and have adapted themselves to the new conditions. And so I am of the opinion that they should be given more time, that they will change even more, that they are on the right track. At any rate, Africa cannot afford, in its own interests and for the sake of its good name, to expel the missionaries. Were it to do so, that would be a lapse into a narrowness and intolerance against which I would have to protest. My hope is that I will be able to use the closing years of my life for more useful things".

After unusually enthusiastic applause the President announces that the council of elders is going to withdraw immediately to conclude the deliberations which it has been holding all through the week. The verdict will be announced at 11 o'clock tomorrow morning.

The Verdict

Saturday, June 7

The hall is full to bursting point just as it was on the day the trial opened. A peculiar kind of excitement hangs over the assembly. In these two weeks opponents and friends of the missions have heard so much both in favour of and to the detriment of the missions. No one knows what decision the elders have reached.

President Sinajina begins to speak, but not about the verdict. "I have a message for you", he says. "The missionaries have asked permission to make a statement before the verdict is announced. This permission has been granted".

Now a lean old man with a long beard and dressed in a white robe mounts the platform. In the solemn voice of a preacher he intones:

"Mr President, like you I am a man without a name. Here I am speaking in the name of all the missionaries represented here and, in a sense, of all the foreign missionaries in Africa. In these past days we have deliberated together and we would like to make the following statement.

"We will accept the judgement, however it may turn out and we will not appeal against it. We are not forcing ourselves on Africa. Were we to be expelled, we would leave the country we love, the country which has become our second home; we would leave in sorrow, but without any ill will. It was Christ who first told us to shake the dust from our feet and depart from a town which would not receive us. To do so would hurt us, for the sake of Africa and of its good people. At the same time, however, we would be convinced that the Church in this continent will carry on living; it will face greater difficulties, but it will also find new, creative solutions to these difficulties. The Gospel seed which we have scattered will continue to grow. Africa cannot ever rid itself of Christianity. If the authorities were to try to get rid of Christianity, we would be able to tell them that they would have the people against them.

"Mr President, we have confidence in the council of elders and we leave it to you to announce the verdict".

The President rises and prepares to speak the words everyone has been waiting to hear for the past year and especially for the past two weeks.

"Ladies and gentlemen, citizens of the world", he begin. "Now, at the time when the discussion should really begin, we have to break off. Until now all that has happened is that the two sides have submitted their opposing views. African custom dictates that we should now get together, go over the whole issue again, reflect on it, look at it 20 times from all angles, formulate it with ever greater precision and finally come to a conclusion acceptable to everyone, a conclusion which would leave no one victorious and no one vanquished. Our way of conducting business allows time to do the work; we allow the food to cook until it is soft. We sleep on a problem in the conviction that tomorrow's sun will bring a new message.

"Unfortunately, in the present case things cannot work out that way both because with such vast numbers of people a genuine discussion is not possible and because journalists from all over the world and the missionaries too are always in a hurry. Even we Africans have begun to measure time. For this reason the council of elders has had to take it upon itself to announce its verdict already. At first, our discussions were difficult but eventually, among ourselves, we reached a verdict and we are all behind the considerations which I will now explain to you.

"The first thing we observe is that we are not called upon to pass sentence on individual missionaries, living or dead. The dead have already been tried by a higher court and as for any individual living missionaries who act improperly, the authorities will take care of them.

"Our task is to make a ruling on the missions as an institution and to settle the question, in general terms, of whether they are beneficial or detrimental to Africa or, using a figure of speech, whether the African body can receive this artificially transplanted organ or whether it will reject it. In fact, the missions were something alien, something forced upon us from outside. We have proverbs to the effect that 'buffaloes all stick together and elephants all stick together' and 'Has anyone ever seen a fish leave the water and live in a tree with the monkeys?'. These are more than just sayings, they are pictorial descriptions of the law of nature. The whites have violated this law; they have crossed seas, deserts and forests to reach us; they have abused our hospitality and have dominated us. At the same time they have fought against and wiped out the religion of our forefathers and have preached to us a God whose origin and language were unknown to us. It now lies within our power to drive these foreign elements away again. The other whites, the colonial masters, have already gone; why shouldn't the missionaries go too? Then we would be by ourselves. That is the first consideration.

"There are, however, other factors to take into account. Once again we have a saying which runs: 'Every child believes the food its mother provides is the best in the world'. Now, in fact, this child is fooling itself; it doesn't know anything else. So God arranges that it is not only satisfied with its food but delighted with it. When it learns that there are other better dishes, it begins to long for them.

"In our view, what counts nowadays is not separation, isolation, spiritual and material impoverishment, but encounter, living together, spiritual and material enrichment. What counts more than anything is unity, the reduction of opposites and of bitterness, the building-up of unity. However much one may stress our African-ness, it has been rightly said that a certain predilection for the foreign and for the foreigner is something typical of an African, who sees even in what is foreign a dimension of himself. Our distinguishing characteristic consists precisely in looking at everything in a critical spirit and accepting what is good, provided that it helps to stimulate our African reality, and not bothering about whether it comes from our forefathers or from our brothers from other countries.

"We owe this attitude of openness, this striving for unity not only to ourselves but also to the organisation which has taken over responsibility for this process — the Organisation for African Unity. On the day the O.A.U. was founded, the President, Haile Selassie, speaking in this palace, said: 'Let us seek our own identity, let us set out on the way towards unity. Our efforts to free our as-yet-unfree brothers from the yoke of colonialism must not give cause for accusations of injustice and they must be free from bitterness. Let us act in accordance with the dignity which we Africans claim for ourselves. We are proud of our qualities, of the advantages we have, of our abilities . . .' Article 2 of our Charter requires expressly that we further international cooperation. Unity, then, is a necessary consequence of this. Africa must become one and for the same reasons we have to work also for the unity of the world.

"This basic attitude looking towards unity has determined the direction of our deliberations. And so, after these long preliminary remarks. I can formulate our verdict briefly thus: The council of elders has resolved to defer judgement on the African missions *sine die*, for an indeterminate period . . .".

This announcement is greeted with spontaneous expressions of surprise, joy and relief on the one side and of indignation and disillusionment on the other. The President continues in the same calm way as before.

"Ladies and gentlemen, you will understand this verdict when you have heard the more detailed reasons for it. Firstly, the phenomenon we know as the missions is so complex that even Solomon in all his wisdom would not have been able to make a clear distinction between the good and the not-so-good. We could, of course, have allotted points to all the arguments of the prosecution and of the defence and then presented you with a mathematical result. But even if we were persuaded that the balance tipped in favour of the missions, this purely quantitative result would not be convincing. For this reason we started from more general principles.

"Like everything in life, the missions too have their light sides and their dark sides. War and peace, force and peaceful, friendly encounter, despair and hope alternate constantly. In spite of this we regard life as worth living. If no individual man is perfect, an institution is even less so. There is no such thing as a perfect traditional society, a perfect revolution, a perfect Africa or even a perfect Church. Hence there is no room for triumph or for despair, there is room only for constructive realism. Christians are familiar with the parable of the tares among the wheat, they know about man's original sin. Our African creation-myths also tell us of a good primeval condition without hunger, sickness or death. Men have ruined this condition by their dissatisfaction, their grumbling and their open disobedience. Since that time we are no longer living in paradise and we have to come to terms with this fact. We may not, therefore, kill a man because he is not perfect nor may we condemn an institution because it contains imperfect elements.

"We must now return for a while to a quantitative way of thinking. We know that it is quite impossible to weigh out exactly the good and bad in an institution such as the missions, to which thousands of people belong and which has been operating for more than a 100 years, but surely everyone can see clearly the direction a judgement in this matter would take. This is the second justification for our verdict. Certainly we must not allow ourselves to forget what was said in the first week, the weighty things that were said, on account of the impressions we received in the second week. Quite plainly, however, the scales are tipped in favour of the good. Among the missionaries there were certainly no criminals, there were many who were slaves to an outdated spirit and many more who, in the depths of their being, were good and were utterly devoted to Africa. There is a lot one can criticise and criticise rightly, but our present-day Africa has almost grown out of this spirit which deserved criticism. That which in the past was bad is dead and gone, that which was good has borne abiding fruit. There are so many extenuating reasons for the mistakes that were made that it is better not to talk about them any more. Without a doubt the final balance would turn out in favour of the misions.

"In spite of this we have not passed sentence but have deferred it indefinitely. This is because we are still too close to the phenomenon we call the missions and it is the third justification for our verdict. As long as one is walking through the jungle, one has no general view. We have to be further away in order to be able to make an objective, comprehensive judgement. Time, the future, history will give the verdict. In his last letter to his wife, Patrice Lumumba wrote: 'One day history will speak its word . . . Africa will write its own history'. This is true in the present case. The mangoes should not be knocked off the tree before they are ripe — only naughty boys do that. Neither unborn nor ageing life should be ended by force but should be allowed to grow until life finds its solution. We have heard that the missionaries are adapting to the new age, that they are declining in numbers. The process we desire is already taking place; let us give it the time it needs. Local Churches may, if they think it a good thing, step up this process. We, as an extra-ecclesiastical court, were of the opinion that we have no right to interfere. In any case, we already know that the missions are waning like the full moon and African Christianity is rising like the sun.

"Historians of the future will, because they are sufficiently far away from these events, be able to make a correct judgement. But time also gives scope for the formation of legends. Legends get at the essence of truth better than does the mere presentation of historical facts. The legends and myths of our ancestors and forebears are of significance to us men of today, both young and old. We believe — and we already have indications that this has begun to happen — that legends will grow around the great pioneering figures of the missions. Those Church-founders of old will edify and inspire today's Christians, many of whom visit the graves of their missionaries and derive strength and hope from so doing. After losing our primeval paradise, all of us, Christians and non-Christians alike, look forward with longing to a paradise in the future — Christians call this the kingdom of God. Of course, everyone is free to believe or not to believe in a future kingdom. Nonetheless, we believe that a hope of this nature does not lull men to sleep but stimulates them, does not alienate them but allows them to become aware of themselves. This is why figures which awaken this hope for us should stand like a monument before our eyes.

"Our judgement must be understood on the basis of all these considerations. On the one hand, it turns against the increased use of force as a solution to problems in an age when we have so many possibilities of dialogue and communication. On the other hand, it aims to encourage the idealism of the young, to get them to engage their lives in great acts of service to mankind wherever and in whatever way such services are needed. Without such acts of service the world and mankind would be much poorer.

"Our judgement can compel no one, but its moral force should not be underestimated. Individual governments have it in their power to expel the missionaries as a group. But then of course they will have to bear the responsibility for having done so. We believe that force should not be used either to impose or to suppress religion, ideas and ideologies. The only thing that counts in this matter is the power of conviction and history will judge this.

"I repeat then: the council of elders has resolved to postpone judgement on the missions in Africa indefinitely. The council will make a report to the O.A.U. And so the missions in Africa will have to wait for their judgement. This waiting will be to their advantage. In the year 2000 one will be able to state with greater authority than we can at present what the missions were and are, and whether the missions — and, if so, which missions — should determine what Africa will look like in the future.

"Ladies and gentlemen, this sitting is now concluded".

BIBLIOGRAPHY

Actes de la 4ème Assemblée plénière du Symposium des Conférences Episcopales d'Afrique et de Madagascar. Texte réservé, Rome, 1975.
African Writers Series, London, Heinemann (over 100 titles).
Ageneau, R., and D. Pryen. *Après la Mission.* Paris, 1975.
All Africa Conference of Churches' Assembly in Lusaka. IDOC-Bulletin, n. 22, 1974.
Ayandele, E. A. *The Missionary Impact on Modern Nigeria.* New York: Humanities Press, 1967.
Baëta, C. G. (ed.). *Christianity in Tropical Africa.* London: Oxford University Press, 1968.
———. *Prophetism in Ghana.* London, 1962.
———. *Survey of the Training of the Ministry in Africa.* London, 1954.
Barrett, D. B. *Schism and Renewal in Africa: An Analysis of Six Thousand Contemporary Religious Movements.* Nairobi: Oxford University Press, 1968.
Beaver, R. P. *The Gospel and Frontier Peoples.* South Pasadena: William Carey Library, 1973.
Becken, H. J. (ed.). *Relevant Theology for Africa.* Durban, 1973.
Beckmann, J. *Die katholische Kirche im neuen Afrika.* Einsiedeln: Benziger, 1947.
Beti, M. *Poor Christ of Bomba.* African Writers' Series. Atlantic Highlands, N.J.: Humanities Press, 1972.
Bischofberger, O. *Tradition und Wandel aus der Sicht der Roman-schriftsteller Kameruns und Nigerias.* Schöneck, 1968.
Bühlmann, W. *Afrika, gestern, heute, morgen.* Herder-Bücherei, 1960.
———. *Die Kirche unter den Völkern: Afrika.* Mainz, 1963.
———. *Wo der Glaube lebt. Einblicke in die Lage der Weltkirche.* Freiburg i. Br., 1974.
———. *The Coming of the Third Church.* Maryknoll, N.Y.: Orbis, 1977.
———. *Courage, Church! Essays in Ecclesial Spirituality.* Maryknoll, N.Y.: Orbis, 1978.
Bürki, B. *L'assemblée dominicale.* Introduction à la liturgie des Eglises protestantes d'Afrique. Immensee: NZM, 1976.
Bürkle, H. *Theologie und Kirche in Afrika.* Stuttgart, 1968.
Butturini, G. (ed.). *Le nuove vie del Vangelio. I vescovi Africani parlano a tutta la Chiesa.* Bologna: EMI, 1975.
Casiraghi, G. *Le nuove società afro-asiatiche.* Bologna: EMI, 1973.
Classiques africains. Paris (15 titles so far).
Cone, J. H. *Black Theology of Liberation.* Philadelphia: Lippincott, 1970.
Dantine, W. *Schwarze Theologie. Eine Herausforderung der Theologie der Weissen?* Vienna, 1976.
Eggen, W. *Peuple d'autrui. Une approche anthropologique de l'oeuvre pastorale en milieu centrafricain.* Brussels: PMV, 1976.
Filesi, T. *La "missio antiqua" dei Cappuccini nel Congo.* Rome, 1977.
Gheddo, P. *Processo alle missioni.* Milan, 1971.
Groves, C. P. *The Planting of Christianity in Africa.* 4 vols. London: Lutterworth, 1948–1958.
Hastings, A. *Church and Mission in Modern Africa.* New York: Fordham, 1967.
——. *African Christianity.* New York: Seabury, 1977.
Hegba, M. P. *Emancipation d'Eglises sous tutelle, Essai sur l'ère post-missionaire.* Paris, 1976.
Hertlein, S. *Mission im Urteil der neoafrikanischen Prosaliteratur.* Münsterschwarzach, 1962.
———. *Wege christlicher Verkündigung,* I. Münsterschwarzach, 1976.
Idowu, E. B. *Towards an Indigenous Church.* London: Oxford University Press, 1965.
Italiaander, R. *Der ruhelose Kontinent.* Düsseldorf, 1958.
———. *Profile und Perspektiven.* Erlangen, 1971.

Jahn, J. *Wir nannten sie Wilde. Aus alten und neuen Resebeschreibungen*. Münich, 1964.
———. *Bibliography of Neo-African Literature*. London: Deutsch, 1965.
———. *History of Neo-African Writing in Two Continents*. London: Faber, 1968.
———. *Jeune Afrique*. Hebdomadaire International Indépendent, Paris.
Luykx, B. *Culte chrétien en Afrique après le Vatican II*. Immensee: NZM, 1974.
Lycops, J. P. *Il genocidio culturale in Africa*. Milan, 1975.
Marie-André du S. Coeur. *La femme noire en Afrique occidentale*. Paris.
———. *La femme noire dans la société africaine*. Paris, 1940.
———. *Ouganda, terre des martyrs*. Paris: Casterman, 1964.
Mbiti, J. S. *African Religions and Philosophy*. New York: Doubleday, 1970.
———. *Concepts of God in Africa*. London: S.P.C.K., 1970.
———. *The Prayers of African Religion*. Maryknoll, N.Y.:Orbis, 1976.
———. *New Testament Eschatology in an African Background*. London: Oxford University Press, 1971.
McEwan, P. J. M. (ed.). *Africa from Early Times to 1800*. London: Oxford University Press, 1968.
———. *Nineteenth-Century Africa*. London: Oxford University Press, 1968.
———. *Twentieth-Century Africa*. London: Oxford University Press, 1968.
Mobley, H. W. *The Ghanaian Image of the Missionary*. Leiden: Brill 1970.
Motlabi, M. (ed.). *Essays on Black Theology*. Johannesburg, 1973.
Mulago, V. *Un visage africain du christianisme*. Paris, 1965.
Nyerere, J. *Freedom and Unity*. Dar es Salaam: Oxford University Press, 1966.
———. *Freedom and Socialism*. Dar es Salaam: Oxford Unversity Press, 1968.
———. *Freedom and Development*. Dar es Salaam: Oxford University Press, 1973.
Okot p'Bitek. *African Religions in Western Scholarship*. Nairobi, 1970.
Oliver, R. *The Missionary Factor in East Africa*. Atlantic Highlands, N.J.: Humanities Press, 1967.
Oosthuizen, G. *Post-Christianity in Africa: Theological and Anthropological Study*. Grand Rapids: Eerdmans, 1968.
———. *Theological Battleground in Asia and Africa: The Issues Facing the Churches and the Efforts to Overcome Western Divisions*. Atlantic Highlands, N.J.: Humanities Press, 1972.
Paul VI, *Africae Terrarum*, Vatican City, 1967.
Présence Africaine. Revue culturelle du monde noir, Paris.
Rees, D. *Soviet Strategic Penetration of Africa*. London, 1976.
Sanon, A. *Tierce-Eglise, ma mère*. Paris, 1970.
Sawyerr, H. *Creative Evangelism: Towards a New Christian Encounter with Africa*. London: Butterworth 1968.
Semaines de Missiologie de Louvain, 1968: *Liberté des jeunes Eglises;* 1971: *Quel missionaire?*
Settimana di Studi Missionari (XIII). *Evangelizzare oggi*. Bologna, 1976.
Shorter, A. *African Christian Theology: Adaptation or Incarnation?* Maryknoll, N.Y.: Orbis Books, 1977.
Singleton, M. *"Let my people go. . .": A Survey of the Catholic Church in Western Nigeria*. Brussels: PMV, 1974.
Sundermaier, T. (ed.). *Christus, der schwarze Befreier*. Erlangen, 1973.
Tasia, G., and R. Gray (ed.). *Christianity in Independent Africa*. London, 1977.
Tchidimbo, R. M. *L'homme noir face au christianisme*. Paris, 1963.
Thomas, L. V., and R. Luneau. *La terre africaine et ses religions*. Paris: Larousse, 1975.
Tshibangu, T. *Le propos d'une théologie africaine*. Kinshasa, 1974.
Various authors. *Des prêtres noirs s'interrogent*. Paris, 1956.
Verryn, T. D. (ed.). *Church and Marriage in Modern Africa*. Johannesburg, 1975.
Verstraelen, F. J. *An African Church in Transition*. Leiden, 1976.
Weyel, V. *Interaktion von Politik und Religion in Uganda nach 1875*. Münich, 1976.